The Way of the Writer

REFLECTIONS *on the* ART *and* CRAFT *of* STORYTELLING

Charles Johnson

SCRIBNER

New York   London   Toronto   Sydney   New Delhi
A Work from the Johnson Construction Co.

SCRIBNER
An Imprint of Simon & Schuster, Inc.
1230 Avenue of the Americas
New York, NY 10020

Copyright © 2016 by Charles Johnson

First Scribner edition December 2016

SCRIBNER and design are registered trademarks of The Gale Group, Inc.,
used under license by Simon & Schuster, Inc., the publisher of this work.

For information about special discounts for bulk purchases,
please contact Simon & Schuster Special Sales at 1-866-506-1949
or business@simonandschuster.com.

The Simon & Schuster Speakers Bureau can bring authors to your live event.
For more information or to book an event, contact the Simon & Schuster Speakers
Bureau at 1-866-248-3049 or visit our website at www.simonspeakers.com.

Manufactured in the United States of America

1   3   5   7   9   10   8   6   4   2

Excerpts from "Burnt Norton," "East Coker" and "Little Gidding"
from FOUR QUARTETS by T. S. Eliot. Copyright 1936 by Houghton Mifflin
Harcourt Publishing Company; Copyright © renewed 1964 by T. S. Eliot.
Copyright 1940, 1942 by T. S. Eliot; Copyright © renewed 1968, 1970
by Esme Valerie Eliot. Reprinted by permission of Houghton Mifflin
Harcourt Publishing Company. All rights reserved.

"A Boot Camp for Creative Writing" first appeared in
The Chronicle of Higher Education on October 31, 2003; "Storytelling
and the Alpha Narrative" was first published in The Southern Review's Winter
2005 issue; and "The Truth-Telling Power of Fiction" was delivered as the plenary
Coss Lecture, "At the Crossroad of Philosophy and Literature" at the 43rd
annual Society for the Advancement of American Philosophy conference
on March 4, 2016, and a shorter version of it was published in
The Chronicle of Higher Education on December 2, 2013.

Library of Congress Cataloging-in-Publication Data is available.

ISBN 978-1-5011-4721-0
ISBN 978-1-5011-4722-7 (pbk)
ISBN 978-1-5011-4723-4 (ebook)

For Dr. Joseph W. Scott,
a restless, relentless seeker of knowledge
about the writing craft.

Contents

Contents

III. What Helps the Writer?

IV. The Writer as Teacher

V. The Writing Life and the Duties of the Writer

Contents

VI. Philosophy and the Writer

Introduction

We shall not cease from exploration
And the end of all our exploring
Will be to arrive where we started
And know the place for the first time.
                                    —T. S. Eliot

At the end of 2010, the poet E. Ethelbert Miller, who was recently inducted into the Washington, DC, Hall of Fame for his contributions to literature and public life, presented me with a proposal that at first glance might have seemed preposterous. He asked if he could interview me for an entire year. Actually, his idea really wasn't all that outrageous because he and I were corresponding daily, e-mailing each other our thoughts and feelings about literary news, politics, and culture. This electronic dialogue no doubt came about because as two black men only two years apart in age, we had traversed the same cultural, intellectual, racial, and political landscape since the 1950s. We had much in common, and Ethelbert was uniquely suited to be the interlocutor in this unusual enterprise of intensely examining a single writer's life and work.

I say this about Ethelbert Miller because it is very difficult to find someone in the writing community, here or abroad, who has not been touched by his unselfish contributions to literary culture since the late 1960s. A *Washington Post* feature on Miller once referred to him as "Mr. 411," the person you contact if you have a question about literary artists in this country. For two generations now, he has devoted himself to the support of other writers, young and old. In the literary world, he is an activist who is as ubiquitous as air—publishing poetry and memoirs, columns and social commentary, chairing the board for the Institute for Policy Studies, a progressive think tank, directing until recently the African American Resource Center at Howard University, and editing *Poet Lore*, the oldest poetry magazine in America. For him art is spirit work aimed at realizing the "beloved community" that Martin Luther King, Jr., envisioned. He works as indefatigably as W. E. B. Du Bois, and his work is always in support of social justice and bringing to the community of literary artists on this continent (and other continents) a spirit of cooperation, not competition; compassion, not indifference; and idealism, not cynicism. He cares about everyone.

So in January 2011 we began the project that the literary scholar Marc Conner, provost at Washington and Lee University, said allows readers "to spend a year in the writer's house." For twelve months, Ethelbert dutifully read my novels, short stories, and essays, and asked me more than four hundred questions about every subject under the sun—literature, meditation, Buddhism, teaching, martial arts, the civil rights movement and Martin Luther King, Jr., contemporary and canonical writers, films, poetry, Sanskrit, my personal habits, American history, technology, sex, race, the state of black America, the love of dogs, science, philosophy, the Culture Wars, comic art and my 1970 drawing show on PBS, *Charlie's Pad*, fatherhood, and the literary world we've both labored in for so long. On and on, the questions came. I answered around 218, my posts growing longer and more detailed, becoming mini-essays, when I realized at some point that Ethelbert had given me an unprecedented opportunity to set the record straight in regard to my thoughts and feelings about a galaxy of subjects I'd studied or reflected on since childhood. Four years after this collaboration these reflections were reborn in the 672-page tome *The Words and Wisdom of Charles Johnson* (Dzanc Books, 2015).

From several readers of *Words and Wisdom*, and from Ethelbert himself, I kept hearing that from the original work a more focused manual on the craft of creative writing and storytelling could be conjured. Slowly but surely, this suggestion began to make sense to me. Over the years, I'd published articles on literary craft, but no book devoted to the subject. After holding the S. Wilson and Grace M. Pollock Endowed Professor of Writing Chair at the University of Washington, directing the creative-writing program, editing the periodical the *Seattle Review* (1978–98), serving on the board of the Associated Writing Programs, and mentoring countless undergraduate and graduate students in fiction writing, I retired from teaching in 2009. For thirty-three years I led a teacher's life, but I'd left no record for those decades of pedagogy.

This book is that record. While I've used on these pages the original essay-posts from 2011, often keeping Ethelbert's original questions as prompts, I've generally revisited them to expand and elaborate on their contents. Five years ago, we conducted our experiment in a creative heat that inspired a relaxed, spontaneous, and conversational feel for the essays.

As I reread my discussions of literary craft with Ethelbert, I realized that I've been widely publishing fiction and nonfiction (and drawings) for fifty-one years, starting in 1965 when I was seventeen. Since high school, I've spent my days and nights immersed in a creative process that is always rewarding because it is an exercise in problem-solving and discovery that utilizes all of one's intellect, emotions, and imagination. If there are rules for writing well, they are at best provisional insofar as each instance of a well-done story teaches us anew what a story can be and the possibilities for invention and innovation. The universe of storytelling is capacious enough to comfortably contain all forms of entertainment, low and high, literary and pulp, transcendent and trashy, visionary and pedestrian (and some works, of course, embody that entire range or continuum of creative expression all at once).

So it has always seemed to me that rigid formulas and rules serve us less well than a certain temperament or natural predisposition. What do I mean by that? I mean, simply, that one must begin with a genuine love of art.

In order to prepare oneself for a life devoted daily to creating—and it is important to envision oneself engaged in this activity day and night, 24/7, until one's last day on Earth—a prerequisite is the joy we experience when discovering and creating something new. That joy, or passion if you like, naturally leads to wanting to know, experience, and understand the creations of others. Like a thread that is pulled on a garment or the limbs of a tree branching out, you are inexorably led from your own individual canvases to the work of others in your field, present and past, from all cultures and countries, all traditions and styles, and all periods of human history, regardless of the race, class, or gender of these creators. The necessity for this is both selfless and selfish, the first just because one loves the experience of beauty (which is a form of truth) wherever one finds it; but there is selfishness here, too, insofar as the catholic exposure to the rich diversity of art, literary or otherwise—art that is our *human* inheritance—expands one's own technical skills for solving problems that creators have universally faced in composing their compositions. The tragedy of "aesthetic" positions based on political or racial ideologies is not merely that they constrict and limit consciousness, nor that they are sadly separatist in a world demonstrably of interconnected-

ness, but rather they are unsatisfactory because they impov
erish the toolbox of ideas, *techne*, and strategies that a prolific
artist must draw from when faced with a lifetime of creating
in many genres and forms.

In *The Educated Imagination*, a series of entertaining and
brilliant radio lectures delivered by the great literary scholar
Northrop Frye on Canadian radio in the 1960s, he observes:

> A writer's desire to write can only have come from pre-
> vious experience of literature, and he'll start by imi-
> tating whatever he's read, which usually means what
> people around him are writing. This provides for him
> what is called a convention, a certain typical and socially
> accepted way of writing. . . . After working in this con-
> vention for a while, his own distinctive sense of form will
> develop out of his knowledge of literary technique. He
> doesn't create out of nothing; and whatever he has to say
> he can say only in a recognizably literary way. We can
> perhaps understand this better if we take painting as our
> example. There have been painters since the last ice age,
> and I hope there'll be painters until the next one: they
> show every conceivable variety of vision, and of origi-
> nality in setting it out. But the actual technical or formal
> problems of composition involved in the act of getting
> certain colors and shapes on a flat surface, usually rectan-
> gular, have remained constant from the beginning.
> So with literature. In fiction, the technical problems
> of shaping a story to make it interesting to read, to pro-
> vide for suspense, to find the logical points where the
> story should begin and end, don't change much in what-
> ever time or culture the story's being told.

Just as the objects we create have certain common charac-
teristics, so too did some of the creators I've been fortunate

to know during my life's journey—John Gardner, my UW colleague Jacob Lawrence, and August Wilson. Writers have a common love (one might also call it a need, like the need we have for food and air) for the creative process, despite the differences in their fields. It's not quite accurate to describe this love, as I like to put it, as being similar to a "career" choice, because it is not something the writer or painter arbitrarily chooses. More accurately, it should be seen as a way of being-in-the-world. As with other things we deeply love and are ready to make sacrifices for, the artist surrenders to it, and to all the demands of a life devoted to creating, which in the case of the writer with an "educated imagination" means the desire to understand both the lives of other artists and the critical history and philosophical foundations from which their works arise. In other words, we find ourselves forever thinking and talking passionately about literary art to better understand what we love (and sometimes dislike), which segues into writing *about* new works (book reviewing), to more formalized reflections and analysis of stories (scholarship), to wanting to share what we have learned about something we love (teaching), and, finally, to encouraging others to add to the body of creations in the fields that are dear to us (by judging contests, publishing others, creating awards for them, and mentoring). It is all one piece, this writing life, and each activity—professional and personal—enriches the others. Everything flows from the same source—the love of art. All art.

For the kind of writer I've just described, what might have been selfish or ego-driven at the onset of his or her career gives way—as is always the case with love—to the simple desire to humbly serve and possibly enrich, if we are lucky, literary culture in our time.

My hope is that, if nothing else, readers young and old, beginners and veterans, will experience on these pages devoted to the craft, the discipline, the calling of writing, that predisposition to love the goodness, truth, and beauty found in fine writing (and all well-wrought art). And to see that serving such a mistress for a lifetime is, in the truest sense of the word, a privilege and a blessing.

Dr. Charles Johnson
Seattle, Washington
January 2016

Who Is the Writer?

1. In the Beginning . . .

People sometimes wonder what a person was like before he or she became a writer. What was that person's childhood like? In my case, I imagine that my being an only child growing up in the 1950s in the Chicago suburb of Evanston, Illinois, in the shadow of Northwestern University, shaped my life in more ways than I can imagine.

I was born on April 23 (Shakespeare's birthday), 1948, at a place I described in my novel *Dreamer*: Community Hospital, an all-black facility. In my novel I renamed this important institution "Neighborhood Hospital," and called the woman who spearheaded its creation, Dr. Elizabeth Hill, by the fictionalized name Jennifer Hale. In the late 1940s, Dr. Hill—one of Evanston's first black physicians—was barred by segregation from taking her patients to all-white Evanston Hospital. Instead, she was forced to take them to a hospital on the South Side of Chicago, and quite a few of her patients died in the ambulance on the way. Almost single-handedly (or so I was told as a child), Dr. Hill organized black Evanstonians (and some sympathetic whites) to create a black hospital. Our family patriarch, my great-uncle William Johnson, whose all-black construction crew (the Johnson Construction Co., which this book honors on its title page) built churches, apartment buildings, and residences all over the North Shore area, would go nowhere else for treatment, even after Evanston Hospital was integrated in the 1950s. And every black baby born to my generation in Evanston came into the world there—my classmates and I all had in common the fact that we had been delivered by Elizabeth Hill. She considered us her "children." Even when I was in my early twenties she knew me by sight and would ask what I'd been up to since I last saw her.

Predictably, then, I grew up in a black community in the 1950s that had the feel of one big, extended family. Ebenezer A.M.E. Church, where I was baptized (and later my son) and married, was a central part of our collective lives. In an atmosphere such as this, everybody knew their neighbors and saw them in church on Sunday; it was natural for grown-ups to keep an eye on the welfare of their neighbors' children and to help each other in innumerable ways. In short, Evanston in the 1950s was a place where, beyond all doubt, I knew I was loved and belonged.

My father worked up to three jobs to ensure our family never missed a meal. We weren't poor, but neither were we wealthy or middle-class. Every so often my mother took a job to help make ends meet, including one at Gamma Phi Beta sorority at Northwestern University, where she worked as a cleaning woman during the Christmas holidays. She brought me along to help because she couldn't afford a babysitter. I remember her telling me that the sorority's chapter said no blacks or Jews would ever be admitted into its ivied halls. My mother brought home boxes of books thrown out by the sorority girls when classes ended, and in those boxes I found my first copies of Mary Shelley and Shakespeare. I read them, determined that the privileged girls of that sorority would never be able to say they knew something about the Bard that the son of their holiday cleaning woman didn't. Decades later in 1990 Northwestern's English department actively and generously pursued me for employment by offering me a chair in the humanities, which I declined.

Along with those books from Northwestern, my mother filled our home with books that reflected her eclectic tastes in yoga, dieting, Christian mysticism, Victorian poetry, interior decorating, costume design, and flower arrangement. On boiling hot Midwestern afternoons in late July when I was tired of drawing (my dream was to become a cartoonist and illustrator), I would pause before one of her many bookcases and pull down a volume on religion, the Studs Lonigan trilogy, poetry by Rilke, *The Swiss Family Robinson*, Richard Wright's *Black Boy*, an 1897 edition of classic Christian paintings (all her books are now in my library), or Daniel Blum's *Pictorial History of the American Theatre 1900–1956*, which fascinated me for hours. She was always in book clubs, and I joined one, too, to receive monthly new works of science fiction when I was in my middle teens. (Believe it or not, I had a hardcover first edition of Philip K. Dick's *The Man in the High Castle*, which I've always regretted letting slip away from me.)

As an only child, books became my replacement for siblings. Exposed to so many realms of the imagination, I vowed to read at least one book a week after I started at Evanston Township High School (from which, by the way, my mother had graduated in the late thirties). I started with adventure stories like those by Ian Fleming and ended my senior year with Plutarch's *Lives of the Noble Grecians*. I spent hours each week at a newsstand selecting the next paperback I'd spend several days of my life with. And, as might be expected, it happened that one week I finished early—on a Tuesday, I recall—and I thought, "God, what do I *do* now with the rest of the week?" So I read a second book. Then it became easy to make it three books a week, and I *did* think—but only once—that someday it might be nice to have my name on the spine of a volume I'd written.

And so, again, ours was a house not just of provocative books but also inexpensive and intriguing (to me) art objects

5

that Mother found at flea markets and rummage sales. When she couldn't find them, she *built* them—for example, wall shelves with interesting designs to hold small figurines. We'd read the same books together sometimes, Mother and me, and discuss them. I think she relied on me for this, even raised me to do it, since my hardworking father had little time for books. She had the soul of an actress, a biting wit, and loved art. She'd always wanted to be a teacher, but couldn't because she suffered from severe bouts of asthma. So she made me her student. Like so many other things I owe to my mother, I am indebted to her for seducing me with the beauty of blank pages—a diary she gave me to record my thoughts. But this was by no means a new infatuation. As with books, it was into drawing that I regularly retreated as a child. There was something magical to me about bringing forth images that hitherto existed only in my head where no one could see them. I remember spending whole afternoons blissfully seated before a three-legged blackboard my parents got me for Christmas, drawing and erasing until my knees and the kitchen floor beneath me were covered with layers of chalk and the piece in my hand was reduced to a wafer-thin sliver.

Something to understand about Evanston in the 1950s and '60s is that, unlike many places, the public schools were integrated. From the time I started kindergarten I was thrown together with kids of all colors, and I found it natural to have friends both black and white. Evanston Township High School, we were constantly reminded, was, at the time, rated the best public high school in the nation. It was a big school, almost like a small college—my graduating class had almost a thousand students; black students made up 11 percent of that population. In its progressive curriculum we found an education provided, clearly, by the wealthy white Evanston parents who sent their children there. I took advantage of all the art and photography, literature and history classes.

And to its credit, ETHS offered a yearly creative-writing class taught by the short-story writer Marie-Claire Davis. At the time she was publishing in the *Saturday Evening Post*. As an aspiring cartoonist, I thought writing stories was fun and I came alive in my literature classes, where we read Orwell, Shakespeare, Melville, and Robert Penn Warren, but writing wasn't the kick for me that drawing was. Regardless, I let a buddy talk me into enrolling in Marie's class with him. We talked to each other the whole time and barely listened to poor Marie. But she put Joyce Cary's lovely book *Art and Reality* in front of us, without discussing it in class, and with the hope that we might read it on our own, which I did, and something in me so enjoyed his essays on art and aesthetics that I thought, yes, someday I'd like to do a book like this, too. (You might say you're holding that book in your hands right now.) When I turned in my three stories for Marie's class in 1965, she rushed them into print in the literary section of our school's newspaper (with my illustrations), which she supervised. I always feel indebted to her. And so in the 1990s I established an award, the Marie-Claire Davis Award, at the high school—$500 for the best senior student portfolio of creative writing. For years before her death, Marie would travel from Florida to shake the hand of the winner of that award.

Inevitably, the passion for drawing led me to consider a career as a professional artist. From the Evanston Public Library I lugged home every book on drawing, cartooning, and illustration, and collections of early comic art (Cruikshank, Thomas Rowlandson, Daumier, Thomas Nast), and pored over them, considering what a wonderful thing it would be—as an artist—to externalize everything I felt and thought in images. Some Saturday mornings I sat on the street downtown with my sketchbook, trying to capture the likenesses of buildings and pedestrians. And I made weekly trips to Good's Art Supplies to buy illustration board with my allowance and money earned from my paper route (and later from a Christmas job working nights until dawn on the assembly line at a Rand McNally book factory in Skokie, and from still another tedious after-school job cleaning a silks-and-woolens store where well-heeled white women did their shopping). Good's was a little store packed to the ceiling with the equipment—the tools—I longed to buy. The proprietor, a fat, friendly man, tolerated my endless and naïve questions about what it was like to be an artist and what materials were best for what projects; he showed me a book he'd self-published on his theory of perspective (I never bought it), and after he'd recommended to me the best paper for my pen-and-ink ambitions, I strapped my purchase onto the front of my bicycle and pedaled home.

For a Christmas present my folks finally did buy me one of Good's drawing tables, new for $25. I made space for it in my bedroom and set it up like a shrine. That table would carry me through two years of drawing furiously for my high school newspaper (my senior year, in 1966, I received two second-place awards in the sports and humor divisions for a comic strip and panel from the Columbia Scholastic Press Association's national contest for high school cartoonists), through my first professional job as an illustrator when I was seventeen—drawing for the catalog of a magic-trick company in Chicago. And then that first drawing table was with me, like an old friend, for the next four years of college when I drew thousands of panel cartoons, political cartoons, illustrations (even the design for a commemorative stamp), and every kind of visual assignment for my college newspaper, for the *Chicago Tribune* (where I interned in 1969, then worked for as a stringer when I returned to college), for a newspaper in southern Illinois, and for many magazines known as the "black press" in that era: *Jet*, *Ebony*, *Black World* (né *Negro Digest*), and *Players* (a black version of *Playboy*), all of which culminated in 1970 when I was twenty-two years old with an early PBS drawing show, *Charlie's Pad*, that I created, hosted, and co-produced.

After that early, exhaustive seven-year career, I was ready to start writing fiction full-time. To tell stories with words and not just visual images.

2. The Apprentice Novels

I wrote six unpublished novels between 1970 and 1972 before my debut novel, *Faith and the Good Thing.*

I came to novel-writing with a background in journalism (my bachelor's degree) and writing for newspapers in Chicago and southern Illinois. Creating copy quickly is something every journalist learns to do, and he (or she) has no problem with filing three or four stories a week. That was the training I brought to novel-writing. I knew I could write ten pages a day, five days a week (taking a break on weekends to relax, do research, and/or rewrite), and thereby produce a three-hundred-page manuscript in ten weeks. My master's thesis, for example, was written over five days, ten pages a day; and, later in life, I typically held myself to a five-page-a-day schedule when writing screen- and teleplays.

The first of those six unpublished novels had the working title *The Last Liberation*, and it was an exploration of Eastern philosophy set in a Chicago kung fu school like Chi Tao Chuan of the Monastery, the *kwoon* I trained at in 1967 during the Chicago "Dojo Wars" when I was nineteen years old. At that age I was only vaguely aware of the war between the teachers in my school and another one, but once it erupted during our class time. I recall one evening a young teacher from that other dojo entering our studio and challenging us to a competition his school was sponsoring. The master of our school wasn't there that evening. But during

our next class, he was. And he told us students that if anyone ever dared to enter our *kwoon* like that again, we were
instructed to take one of the weapons off the wall and kill
him—and that we were legally in our rights to do so because
he was trespassing. This *was* a rough martial arts school, one
that operated before the adoption of safety rules, where I saw
students knocked out regularly. As beginners, we were timed
on our ability to throw forty-five punches in ten seconds (to
the front, back, and sides) and our skill at fighting three oppo-
nents at once. To show their contempt for other schools, our
teachers started beginners off with black belts. (Little wonder
that other dojos felt they had to go to war with our studio.)
I wondered some nights if I'd be killed myself, but I didn't
care about the danger. All I wanted to do was train. And train
I did, receiving a double promotion on the night of my first
rank test, primarily for my instinctive approach to sparring,
which the master of the school told his instructors looked like
the footwork used by Pa Kua fighters.

The second book was an early version of *Middle Passage*,
that is, written as the log kept by a white captain on a slave
ship. (The research for that was done during a black history
course I took as an undergraduate.) The third novel was a
black family drama. The fourth, fifth, and sixth novels were
a 959-page trilogy (I was shooting for 1,000 pages—a young
man's folly—but ended it early so my wife and I could spend
some quality time together) about the childhood, young man-
hood, and middle age of a black musician. He was a pianist. I
took lessons on the piano around that time with a black friend
who was a musician and in the music department at Southern
Illinois University. (For years we always had a piano in our
home in Seattle, first so I could sometimes practice, then for
my kids when they had music lessons.)

All these early books were written quickly, and before I
learned the proper approach to revising literary fiction. Each

taught me something different. In the first, I felt the characterization was weak. So I focused on improving that in the second novel, where description, as it turned out, was not as strong as I wanted it to be. In the third novel, I worked to improve descriptive passages. In the fourth, fifth, and sixth books I focused on eliminating any of the deficiencies I discovered in the first three. After these experiments, and when I first met John Gardner in the fall of 1972 and put those manuscripts on his desk, he remarked, "What do you want from me? You can write." Yes, I knew that. But I told JG that what I needed at that time from him was a deeper grasp of rhythm and voice. "Oh!" he said. "I can help you with *that*." He was telling the truth, of course, because he was skillful at narrative ventriloquism. Just reading his early short stories would sensitize an apprentice to the possibilities of voice. And, as an exercise I did on my own one afternoon, I copied by hand the first chapter of his second novel, *The Wreckage of Agathon*, the doing of which immediately plunged me into the meter and rhythm of his prose, so much so that even though I didn't know what the content of a sentence would be before I turned the page and looked at it, I could feel from within how it must sound, what its music and length should be. And how interesting it was, I thought, that so many of his short stories ended with three hard stresses, like the slamming of a door.

There is a story I can tell about book four in this series of what I call "apprentice novels" that might be worth sharing. The book, about the childhood of a musician, was accepted in early 1973 for publication by a new, start-up company in New York when I was only a couple of chapters into writing *Faith and the Good Thing*. I was faced with a dilemma. Every young writer wants to be published. But *what* one first publishes is important for one's career. There was no certainty I would publish *Faith* when it was done (or even if I could finish it), but here with one of the earlier manuscripts was a "bird in the hand," so to speak. The publishers liked it because, as they said, it reminded them of the writing of James Baldwin. I felt torn, for with *Faith* I'd found for the first time the beginnings of my own voice and vision, as well as a way to deploy large amounts of philosophy in a work of fiction. With that still nascent book, I'd moved far beyond the earlier six novels.

John Gardner was looking over my shoulder during the nine months (October 1972 through June 1973) I wrote *Faith* (he was the only creative-writing teacher I'd had since Marie-Claire Davis when I was a junior in high school), so I asked him, "What do *you* think I should do?"

His answer was wise: "If you think that later you're going to have to climb over the earlier book, don't publish it."

I say his answer was wise because a debut novel tends to define a young writer. Reviewers look at it and think, "Okay, this shows us what he can do and can't do. Here are his strengths and limitations and, rightly or wrongly, they tell us what to expect from him in the future." It's important, I believe, for a literary writer's first book to be what I call a "performance novel," a demonstration of all the skill and craft he (or she) has learned up to the time of that book's publication. Furthermore, James Baldwin had his own particular vision of life; in 1973 I was developing my individual and literary sense of the world, with its own vocabulary and grammar. I had no interest in being judged imitative. So, after taking the deepest of breaths, I wrote to the publisher and withdrew that fourth novel (yes, that *was* painful to do), gambling that *Faith* would turn out well, which I suppose it did, because thirty-seven years later it is still in print.

The world will never see the inedita I wrote in those two years. That's why I call them "apprentice novels"—they were, in my view, simply preparations for the work that would come later. And on this subject I've always had a strong, perhaps unconventional gut feeling, especially when I think about the roughly seven years or so that Ralph Ellison devoted to composing *Invisible Man*.

Many working novelists publish a book roughly or on average every two years, producing around six garden-variety books over a period of twelve years. That's one approach, if one is primarily concerned with a career and/or writing novels to make money. But if one's goal is to enrich literary culture, a different approach—one I prefer—might instead be to aim at producing over six or seven years *one* many-splendored, fully imagined, and deeply felt novel that has the complexity, density, and polyvalence of six books, and becomes an American cultural artifact like Ellison's novel.

If there is a moral that can be extracted from my Gardner story, it is something I remember a smart young editor telling an audience at one of the Associated Writing Program conferences in the 1980s. He said that publishing is not a democracy. It is an aristocracy. Not everyone, he said, can be published. And authors should not publish their first novels. Writers, he added, should keep in mind that not being published is not failure. And, most important of all, when writers think about their work, they should try to keep in mind the "big picture," that is, seeing each book as being an essential part of a life's work or oeuvre.

3. A Day in the Life

The intellectual world of my time alienated me intel-
lectually. It was a Babel of false principles and blind
cravings, a zoological garden of the mind, and I had
no desire to be one of the beasts.

— George Santayana

My day is the reverse of what a day is for most people. Typically, I'm up working all night until five or six a.m., the same
kind of schedule kept by Descartes and Balzac. How did I
fall into a lifestyle like this? The happiness and well-being
of my family has always been of greater importance to me
than anything else in the social world; in one way or another,
everything I do is for my family. Forty years ago I felt reluc-
tant to work on my creative projects until all the needs of my
wife and children (and now grandson) had been attended to.
It may sound strange for a writer to talk so fervently about
family, but I've always taken to heart the advice given by the
spiritual teacher Eknath Easwaran in his lovely little pam-
phlet *Instructions in Meditation*. There, he wrote:

> Our emphasis on the family context is because it gives
> us countless possibilities every day for expanding our
> consciousness by reducing our self-will or separateness.
> When we are dwelling on ourselves we are constricting

our consciousness. To the extent that we put the welfare of others first, we are able to break out of the prison of our own separateness. . . . This does not mean following the wishes of the other person always, but when it seems necessary to differ, it must be done tenderly and without the slightest trace of resentment or retaliation.

My kids would finally be in bed by nine or ten p.m. So in the quiet, wee hours of the morning, when the phone isn't ringing and there are no errands to run or other distractions, I can concentrate fully for hours at a time. I get up at noon or by one p.m. PST so I can reply to any urgent messages or e-mails from my agents or editors (or anyone) on the East Coast before two p.m. (or five p.m. their time, the end of their business day). Afternoons and evenings are structured around my workout schedule, which is my priority to maintain health and fitness, especially now that I'm sixty-two. On Sunday, Tuesday, and Thursday I lift weights (my bench press is at 280 pounds) for an hour in the early afternoon and, once a week, I practice my Choy Li Fut empty-hand and weapons kung fu sets and tai chi chuan sets with old friends I've trained with since 1981 (since my early twenties I have believed in the traditional Japanese concept of *bunburyodo*—also favored by the writer Yukio Mishima—which literally means "the pen and the sword in accord," literary and martial arts together. For readers interested in more of this, the *Journal of Asian Martial Arts*, volume 9, number 4 (2000), contains the article "Fist of Fantasy: Martial Arts & Prose Fiction—A Practitioner's Prejudices" by James Grady, author of *Six Days of the Condor*, who examines martial art stories by me—"China" and "Kwoon"—and David Hunt, Adam Hall, Jay McInerney, and Peter O'Donnell, and contains two photos of a younger me practicing Eagle Claw technique on a partner and doing a traditional Chinese staff set); on Monday and Wednesday I get on our treadmill for one hundred minutes. (No workouts on Friday and Saturday, my rest days.)

With the day's workout out of the way, my body is completely relaxed and I'm then free to run errands for my family and friends, eat a light meal, and settle into whatever creative work is in progress while others sleep.

Around eight or nine p.m. I usually take a brief nap to reboot my brain, then eat a proper "dinner" at ten. Then I'm leisurely back to work again until dawn—reading, answering correspondence, writing, studying Sanskrit (I'm in my thirteenth year now), practicing meditation, with our dogs, Nova and Biggie, to keep me company in my second-floor study. Naturally, this schedule goes straight out the window when I'm on the road for a speaking engagement or have an early morning meeting. That, of course, never makes me happy. I'm willing to make sacrifices during the creative process. But that very process is shored up and strengthened when we do all we can to have a balanced approach to maintaining fitness in mind, body, and spirit.

4. The Writing Space

Just as people who seriously practice meditation have a room or space in their home dedicated to that activity, so, too, writers (or artists) greatly need a location set aside specifically for the practice of their craft. A place that spiritually puts them in the mood to create.

In 1993, my wife and I remodeled our one-story home, adding a second floor, and we worked with two architects who designed the rooms to our specifications (we wanted lots of bookshelf space, but—sigh—quickly ran out of that). They built for me a second-floor study/office at the rear of the house, a carpeted room with a sliding glass door that opens onto a deck overlooking our backyard of apple, plum, and pear trees.

Two walls of this room have floor-to-ceiling bookshelves. Two walls also have an L-shaped workbench on which sits the PC I'm writing on right now; there's a printer, a copy machine, a drawing table with a glass surface so it can also function as a light box, and other office supplies. Amiddle-most this room is the first piece of furniture I purchased when we moved to Seattle in 1976—a big wooden schoolhouse teacher's desk with many drawers. (Everything I've written since that year has been composed on this scarred desk, on which sits a mahogany version of Thomas Jefferson's laptop desk; I also have in one corner of my study a walnut reproduction of Jefferson's spinning book stand.) The hundreds of books in my study are, naturally, the ones about Western and Eastern philosophy I refer to most often, along with Sanskrit, Pali, and English dictionaries (*The Compact Edition of the Oxford English Dictionary* and *Webster's New Twentieth Century Dictionary*). Also there is a full set of the *World Book Encyclopedia* my parents got for me in 1956 when I was eight years old, which I've never been able to part with (I love reading those old entries).

The walls of this room, which I suppose you could call my man cave, are covered with the awards, degrees (middle school through the PhD in philosophy), and honorary degrees I've received. Four crammed filing cabinets contain manuscript copies of everything I've written or published since 1965. Another four contain my pens and tools for drawing, research on Buddhism, and news articles (as well as science articles) I clip every day, which I feel I may make use of in future writing, fiction or nonfiction. On the door is a copy of Carl Sagan's "Cosmic Calendar" tracing the history of the universe in 365 days (one second equals 430 years), and a wooden plaque that reads THOU SHALT NOT WHINE; and on the back of that door is a poster of the Milky Way galaxy. There is also a framed dollar bill dating back to 1965 when at age seventeen I made my first professional sale as an illustrator; I did six drawings for the catalog of a magic trick company in Chicago, and oh how tempted I often was to spend it during times when I was dead broke, but I'm so glad I never did.

On one wall below a clock and above a big calendar (on which I scribble appointments) hangs a green blackboard on which I write in chalk my daily to-do list (writing deadlines, deadlines for doing student recommendations, etc.) And there are many photos on the walls—one of Richard Wright in his Paris study, standing before a wall of books, one hand on his typewriter, the other in his suit coat pocket; a big photo of Edmund Husserl, the father of phenomenology, which I've had since graduate school; a painting of Jesus my mother once had; photos of myself, Ralph Ellison, and my editor Lee Goerner at the 1990 National Book Awards ceremony when *Middle Passage* won the fiction prize, and of John Gardner (one full bookshelf in this room contains every scholarly book and work of fiction he published). Framed copies of Buddhist *gatha* (prayers and vows) line the walls, as well as a page of color cartoons (with an essay) I published in the *Seattle Times* in 2004 to celebrate Martin Luther King, Jr.'s birthday.

Some objects in my study have a little stick-on label on them in Sanskrit (Devanagari characters) to help me memorize vocabulary every day. (*Dipika* is on my desk lamp.) And there are small statues everywhere—of Martin de Porres (whom my mother loved), St. Francis, Aristotle, Dante, Mark Twain, the Greek god Apollo, Martin Luther King, Jr., Bodhidharma, small plastic figurines of Barack and Michelle Obama, and a small bronze sixteenth-century Burmese statue of Shakyamuni Buddha I purchased in Thailand in 1997 (this gorgeous artwork was made before this nation existed). On my desk, too, sits an orrery; a circular Tibetan prayer wheel; miniatures of the Mars *Spirit* rover and da Vinci's famous flying machine; a small piece of a real meteorite; and a little statue of Disney's Scrooge McDuck. There are stacks of the science magazines for laypeople that I subscribe to (*Science News*, *New Scientist*, *Discovery*, *Science*, published weekly by the American Association for the Advancement of Science, etc.), popular Buddhist publications I publish my work in, and a soft mat my dog Nova sleeps on when he's not curled up under my desk. (He's on it right now.)

One wall displays a death mask (today we call this a "life cast") of my face made by Willa Shalit, who also made one on the same day for the late artist Jacob Lawrence at University Book Store in Seattle during one of her book tours. (You can see photographs of the life casts she did for Richard Nixon, Muhammad Ali, Richard Burton, Federico Fellini, Sophia Loren, Paul Newman, Sammy Davis, Jr., Whoopi Goldberg, Rosa Parks, and many others in her book *Life Cast: Behind the Mask*, Beyond Words Publishing, 1992.)

There is more here, but you get the picture. Over the decades, I've worked in all kinds of environments—on a kitchen table in graduate student housing, in my parents' basement, and in a cramped, roach-infested two-room efficiency apartment on Long Island, NY, that I lived in during one summer in the 1970s when I was broke. That place was rather like a prison cell. But when I'm working, the world around me simply falls away. Obviously, we can't always choose where we're going to create. I've known writers who prefer to work in a noisy café or during a long train ride. But today my study is, obviously, a projection or externalization of my own mind and spirit: a cluttered catastrophe of books, creative tools, memorabilia, and images where I always feel most at home.

5. The Artist as Shape-Shifter

Between 1969 and 1972, I did several book-length cartoon manuscripts. Johnson Publishing in Chicago (the *Ebony, Jet, Black World* people) published the first one, *Black Humor* (1970), which I drew in one intense week after hearing a campus lecture by Amiri Baraka; and a fly-by-night West Coast publisher, Aware Press, did the second, *Half-Past Nation Time* (1972), but after that book came out, its publisher disappeared into thin air with a third book-length manuscript of drawings I did devoted entirely to the subject of slavery. (This second book from 1972 is extremely hard to find, and I have only one copy of it myself.) Yet another book-length manuscript (unpublished) was on meditation and Eastern philosophy—some of those illustrations appear in a little book called *Buddha Laughing* (Bell Tower, 1999), which the editors at *Tricycle: The Buddhist Review* put together. (These drawings were published in that volume shortly before I started writing essays for *Tricycle* and later was selected to be one of their contributing editors by the publisher, Helen Tworkov, just before she stepped down from running that magazine.)

The two published cartoon volumes deal a lot with black cultural nationalism, which was very much with us (tyrannically so, in my opinion) in the late 1960s and early '70s. Critics are right to point out that emphasis in the drawings, and to note the absence of that now dated subject in my fiction and nonfiction.

From my days as an undergraduate forward, my work has always been very interdisciplinary. One form of artistic and intellectual expression nurtures and feeds the others. Whatever it is we call creativity and the imagination—those two great mysteries—can be for some creators experienced as "global" in their lives, not localized in a single form of expression but rather spreading or spilling from one genre to another, one artistic or intellectual discipline to another, for all the humanities (along with the sciences) are related, interconnected. When some people wake up each day they're as liable to pick up a drawing pen as to begin a new story on their word processor, as likely to grapple with a philosophical essay about the mind/body problem as they are with the first stanza of a poem. Magnificent examples of this polyvalence can be seen in *The Writer's Brush: Paintings, Drawings, and Sculpture by Writers*, edited by Donald Friedman (Mid-List Press, 2007). (Frankly, for a Buddhist, one's daily life itself can be seen as a canvas, a work in progress shaped by each and every one of our creative and rational deeds until the day of our death.) One can see creative imagination as the roots and trunk of a tree that shoots forth many branches of expression that arise from the same mysterious, inexhaustible source.

(And isn't there something very quintessentially American, even Emersonian and Ellisonian, about an individual artist—or any person—who embodies the Many in the One, who is creatively free in a democratic republic to do *this* and *this* and, naturally, *that*, too?)

However, for the sake of convenience, people in general—and not just critics—often label or categorize an artist. (This is especially true for artists of color.) We like to put things in neat little boxes. After his or her name, we'll say "novelist," and ignore the other fields in which that individual works. Or we'll say "poet." Or "screenwriter." All of this speaks to the natural, inevitable, and annoying human tendency to oversim-

plify people and things (or any phenomenon) to make them
manageable. I would also say that real art is an aesthetic experience before it is anything else. To approach the artwork *only*
in terms of its sociological, historical, political, or any other
single valence is to reduce and one-dimensionalize that work.
It is to grasp it only for its *utility*, and that is the approach of
a philistine. A polymorphous creator doesn't want to see any
of his children slighted or ignored. (However, that's a situation he or she may simply have to learn to live with.) A sort
of *ars poetica* statement I was asked to write for the Academy
of Arts and Letters when I received its Academy Award in
Literature in 2002 best expresses, metaphorically, how I see
this situation in respect to my own work. Here is a slightly
abbreviated (and updated) version of that statement:

I see my body of work as being like a mansion with
many rooms. The foundation for the mansion is the
novel *Oxherding Tale*. Inside this imaginative "house"
are rooms you can wander through or dwell in for a
while. One has novels. Another has short fiction. A
third has more than three hundred interviews from
radio and television, newspapers, and scholarly journals.
In the fourth you'll find screen- and teleplays. A fifth
has philosophical essays such as "Reading the Eightfold
Path." A subroom of that has essays on many subjects—
on Indonesia, how to draw political cartoons, the craft
of storytelling, a pedagogy for writing workshops, the
history of black cartoonists, an overview of black literature since the Harlem Renaissance, film critiques, and
critical appreciations of many writers. Yet another room
is devoted to book reviews. Another has children's literature and a 2016 calendar celebrating the achievements
of black scientists. Other rooms have editorial and panel
cartoons, comic strips, texts for studio photo books, and

many public addresses and lectures. On and on through this house, from the basement to the attic, you'll find prose and visual art in numerous aesthetic forms (the slave narrative, the sea adventure story, the folk tale, the animal fable, the fabliau, the political novel). There is fiction and nonfiction on the martial arts, affirmative action, "exchange value," Dr. Martin Luther King's refrigerator, and a future in which the government taxes people's dreams, as well as traditional fables and parables in a subroom of the bigger room devoted to short stories. This is my conception of what a *total* body of work should be, one that is evolved over a lifetime, is generous in form and content, and offers a variety of different aesthetic experiences.

6. The Question of Vision

An artist is not paid for his labor but for his vision.
—James Abbott McNeill Whistler

I've spent my entire adult life thinking about and working on the issue of literary and philosophical vision in my oeuvre. All the things I've created, and the various disciplines I've studied, were part of a very conscious, systematic effort to create an interdisciplinary, multicultural body of work that is broad and deep, inventive and expansive. If we are speaking of philosophical vision in all its fullness, we expect it to exhibit three things: coherence, consistency, and completeness.

In our conscious experience, as one profile or appearance (of an object or subject) is called forth, the others recede from view. Thus to *reveal* (a meaning) is also to *conceal* (other meanings), or at least this is so in phenomenological aesthetics. (No, I'm not talking here about that old creative-writing chestnut that says writers should "show" and not "tell" but addressing a deeper issue involving the perspectival nature of perception.) To describe an object (to *say*) is also to *show*. But that saying or showing renders other things unseen or "invisible." In terms of intellectual and creative practice, and the expectations we traditionally have for "men of letters," what that means in terms of my work is that I've attempted to show as many profiles (meanings) as possible across creative works that span novels, short stories, essays, literary criticism, literary journalism, screen- and teleplays, drawings, and so on. (If I have not written about a subject, there is a very strong possibility that I have drawn something about it.) But we know the field in which meanings unfold has an ever-receding horizon. In other words, we shall as historically situated subjects never be able to describe *all* possible profiles or meanings for *any*thing. (And that ensures that life will always be surprising and full of the unexpected.)

However, I have worked during my lifetime at consciously trying to disclose as many profiles of racial and cultural phenomena as I can. And my current interest in science fiction— stories such as "Popper's Disease," "Sweet Dreams," "Guinea Pig," the Emery Jones adventures that I co-author (and illustrate) with my daughter—arises specifically from the need to make a greater presence for contemporary science and technology in my body of work, because phenomena seen from the standpoint of the various sciences reveal a unique meaning.

In one of my writer's notebooks, I came across this statement I jotted down for myself: "If a writer presents only one side of a problem, one meaning in exclusion to all the others, then that writer is guilty of oversimplification, one-dimensionality, a lack of depth, and an act of violence to the phenomenon itself. He has *denied* its richness, scaled down the possibilities of being, frozen the process of meaning at a single fixed point, and cheated the efflorescence of meaning. His (or her) work may be emotionally powerful, it may be rhetorically strong, but it does not have the integrity of real thought, which presents an open-ended series of phenomenological profiles, the light as well as the dark." I feel comfortable with standing by that statement.

Something else that should be said is that, in my humble opinion, a body of work should deliver both theory and practice. An example? The way Richard Wright's novels and stories are complemented by his classic essay "A Blueprint for

Negro Writing" (1937). Thus, you will find stories and visual art in my oeuvre alongside works that are theoretical (*Being and Race*, "Philosophy and Black Fiction," "A Boot Camp for Creative Writing," "Whole Sight," "Storytelling and the Alpha Narrative," even a very early 1973 article I wrote and illustrated entitled "Creating the Political Cartoon"), that is, philosophical and critical books, essays, and articles that clarify the aesthetic principles that are the foundation for artistic practice. I recall decades ago my dear literary agent Anne Borchardt asking me "why" I was writing *Being and Race: Black Writing Since 1970*. Her question was reasonable. Creative writers seldom write works concerned with aesthetics. But my reason for doing it was that, in addition to it being my PhD dissertation, we lacked in our literature a phenomenological aesthetics applied to works of black fiction.

It is truly my hope that when scholars and students (or general readers) examine my body of work they will find interpretations (or creative renditions) that cover a wide range of subjects; they should be able to find *some*thing that addresses ontology or metaphysics, the nature of (Buddhist) perception, the nature of the self, theory of knowledge, politics and race and culture, aesthetics, theory of language, ethics, religion, American history, etc., etc.

In his introduction for *Charles Johnson: The Novelist as Philosopher* (2007), in the section entitled "Charles Johnson and Western Philosophical Traditions," the literary scholar Marc Conner remarks, "Johnson has long been intimately engaged with the very roots of Western philosophical thought: the pre-Socratics, those Greek thinkers who preceded the great age of Socrates, Plato, and Aristotle by several generations. . . . Intriguingly, when it comes to the more famous successors to the pre-Socratics, Plato and Aristotle, Johnson's engagement is much diminished. This is not surprising: for Plato's adherence to rationalism and idealism, and

Aristotle's adherence to empiricism and realism, are neither particularly sympathetic to Johnson's own thought." When I read those words by Dr. Conner, I realized and had to confess that he was right. I've worked with Heraclitus and Parmenides far more often than I have with Plato or Aristotle (and for reasons that he carefully explains). But this "diminished" presence in my body of work, this intellectual weakness, if you will—and Marc pointing that out— mildly annoyed me. So to clear up this matter, I wrote in 2007 a short story entitled "The Cynic," a tale narrated by Plato, who speaks at length about his teacher, Socrates, Diogenes, and many other philosophers. Aristotle even makes a cameo appearance as a young student of Plato. In other words, Dr. Conner's critique inspired me to make an effort to fill in this obvious intellectual and creative gap in my body of work.

For years now I've expressed (to myself) my particular literary vision in a single phrase that joins together East and West, the ancient and the modern, the rigorously philosophical and the spiritual: phenomenological Buddhism. Or perhaps one might say, whimsically, Bodhi-drama.

And is there more to say on this subject of vision? Well, yes, of course. Much more. But let me conclude with yet another notation from my writer's workbook: "Any discipline or field at any moment has areas where it is both strong and weak, and it is the latter that always makes discovery, innovation, and creativity possible. There are areas in any field that are gray, weak, inconclusive, unthematized, 'invisible,' and uncertain in development—this is a guarantee that a significant contribution can be made in that field."

The Process of Writing

7. A Boot Camp
for Creative Writing

If our furniture was as poorly made as our fiction, we would always be falling onto the floor.

—John Gardner

One of my life's great ironies is that, while I've taught in a distinguished creative-writing program for thirty-three years at the University of Washington (we have three MacArthur Fellows in a faculty of nine), I've never taken a college writing workshop, nor did I want to in the 1970s. Back then, when I first began furiously writing fiction, the last thing I wanted to do, as a graduate student moving through rigorous philosophy seminars toward a PhD, was sit through the intellectually questionable workshops I'd seen from a distance or heard about. To my eye, they were dominated by the instructor's personality and unsolicited political opinions, and took an approach that was highly subjective, a "touchy-feely" urging of twentysomethings to "write about what they know." My sense was that those apprentices, who knew so little about literature, history, philosophy, or culture, wrote and rewrote the same underwhelming story, usually about their first sexual experiences, all semester long. Here was not where I wanted to bring my manuscripts. I knew I would be bored. I asked myself then, as I sometimes do now: How long would Melville, Poe, Kafka, Emerson, or Dostoyevsky have survived in a soft-at-the-center course like this?

But when I was hired at the University of Washington in 1976, two years after I published my first novel, *Faith and the Good Thing*, I was faced, at age twenty-eight, with the task of deciding what I thought a heuristic, highly productive fiction workshop should be. From the start, I felt it should be a labor-intensive "skill acquisition" course, emphasizing the sequential acquisition of fiction techniques and providing the opportunity to practice them. The curriculum should be capacious, allowing for instruction in all styles, genres, and subgenres of fiction. I believed that apprentices learned best (as in music or the martial arts) through old-fangled imitation of master craftsmen, through assignments aimed at learning a repertoire of literary strategies, and by writing and revising prodigiously. I saw the goal of a (literary) art class as the creation of artists who were technicians of form and language; it was the preparation of journeymen, not one-trick ponies, who one day would be able to take on any narrative assignment—fiction or nonfiction, screenplay or radio drama, novel or literary journalism—that came up in their careers. And such a class should make clear that writing well was always the same thing as thinking well.

Fortunately, when I first worked out this course for graduate and undergraduate students (for the graduates I simply added stiffer requirements), I had many pedagogical and professional experiences to draw on. I'd spent seven years as a journalist and cartoonist working in all forms, I'd written seven novels, I'd consumed a whole library's worth of writing manuals and texts on aesthetics, and I'd apprenticed with the late novelist John Gardner, a bluff, combustible, and brilliant teacher who once told an interviewer, "Writing is the only religion I have." I remember when he was going over one of my chapters for *Faith* in his office at Southern Illinois University and I asked if he needed to stop in order to prepare for his creative-writing workshop. Gardner shook his mane of silver hair and said, "No, teaching creative writing is a joke," and we continued with his critique of my work until the bell rang for him to go to class.

Because I did not want my short-fiction workshops to be "a joke," I designed them to be demanding, and, though requirements have evolved over the years, their rigor remains the same. I assign three full-length stories for my students to complete and revise during the term. I tell them I don't care what they write, only how they write. If their first story is told in the first person, I ask them to try the other two in the third or second person; and, if their protagonists in that first story are people very much like themselves, to switch their characters' gender, race, or cultural orientation.

I also urge them to experiment with the wealth of literary forms that are our global inheritance as writers. From John Gardner's first book, *The Forms of Fiction* (1962), I extracted a three-page handout entitled "Short Fictional Forms," which shows the essential differences in the sketch, fable, parable, yarn, tale, and modern short story. I give students several other handouts as well, some deadly serious, others more whimsical, including Mark Twain's risible essay "Fenimore Cooper's Literary Offenses"; Lajos Egri's chart "The Bone Structure" from *The Art of Dramatic Writing* (1946), for conceiving well-rounded characters; and my own essay "A Theory for This Course," in which I insist that the work they turn in must present: (1) a story with logically plotted sequences; (2) three-dimensional characters—that is, real people with real problems; (3) sensuous description, or a complete world to which readers can imaginatively respond; (4) dialogue with the authenticity of real speech; (5) a strong narrative voice; (6) rhythm, musicality, and control of the cadences in their fiction; (7) and, finally, originality in theme and execution.

But that is just the beginning of what I ask for.

During the course I have students read Northrop Frye's lovely *The Educated Imagination* to help them see, in my paraphrasing of Kant, that education without imagination is empty, and imagination without education is blind. I lecture on plot, description, dialogue, character, the structure of dramatic scenes, and so forth, but usually from a philosophical angle—for example, tracing the rise of twentieth-century subjectivism and the historical and cultural evolution of viewpoint from the loss of faith in omniscient narrators and an agreed-upon "objective" world to stream of consciousness, the recognition of the relativity of viewpoints, and the preference of many contemporary readers for the supposedly greater authority of first-person narratives. Always, I return students from theory to practice. I give them the impossible task of handing in a photocopy of the finest prose passage they've ever read, telling me in one page why they admire it and what literary strategies in it they want to master. (I promise them that by the end of the term I'll show them how to achieve such effects.) Using the notebooks of Nathaniel Hawthorne and Albert Camus as examples, I ask them to maintain a writer's workbook, one they are to fill daily with images, ideas, scraps of language, character sketches, overheard dialogue, and so forth, that they can use when revising their fiction.

In this creative "boot camp," as I often call it, I always give students a healthy dose of Gardner. (I put everyone who works with me for the first time, grad or undergrad, through the same drill.) When he heard I'd been hired at UW, Gardner sent me three unpublished pages of challenging writing exercises he'd worked out in 1976 for his students at the State University of New York at Binghamton, along with a sobering two-page introduction stating how apprentices must "learn the feeling from within of a complete fictional form," as well as "scores of ways of doing everything." Those exercises and their introduction appear at the end of his posthumously published handbook, *The Art of Fiction* (1984). In the 1970s and '80s, I assigned all thirty exercises to my students, which meant they did three a week. (These days for a class that meets twice weekly I assign the ten most challenging exercises.) Among my favorites, then and now, are:

(1) Write three effective long sentences: each at least one full typed page (or 250 words), each involving a different emotion (for example, anger, pensiveness, sorrow, joy). Purpose: control of tone in a complex sentence.

(2) Describe a character in a brief passage (one or two pages) using mostly long vowels and soft consonants (*o* as in "moan," *e* as in "see"; *l, m, n, sh*, etc.); then describe the same character using mostly short vowels and hard consonants (*i* as in "sit"; *k, t, p, gg*, etc.). The purpose of this exercise, Gardner wrote, is to help the student see that "describing a scene in mostly long vowels and soft consonants achieves an effect far different from that achieved by a passage mostly in short vowels and hard consonants."

(3) Write a monologue of at least three pages in which the interruptions—pauses, gestures, descriptions, etc.—all clearly and persuasively characterize, and the shifts from monologue to gesture and touches of setting (as when the character touches some object or glances out the window) all feel rhythmically right. Purpose: to learn ways of letting a character make a long speech that doesn't seem boring or artificial. (Later, in a second monologue, students present a philosophical position they tend to favor, but present it through a character and in a context that modifies or undermines it.)

Since 1976, my serious students have sparked to this syllabus. Among my earliest apprentices in the late 1970s and early '80s were David Guterson, author of *Snow Falling on Cedars*, and Gary Hawkes, author of several novels, among them *Semaphore* and *Surveyor*. They were burning to write and be artistically challenged. Some students transformed certain exercises, such as Gardner's three-page monologue, into complete stories and published them in literary magazines.

Clearly, with good students, one can be demanding. I urge them, since writers are lovers of language, to begin reading a good dictionary from A to Z (*The Compact Edition of the Oxford English Dictionary* or the 2,129-page, unabridged *Webster's New Twentieth Century Dictionary*, as Gardner and I, respectively, had done, to improve their vocabularies and develop their own lexicons), and my very best students do that. In class, I write a new word each day on the blackboard to see if students know it—*ullage, gride, yirn*, or *kalokagathia*—and give a "prize" (usually a copy of a literary journal) to the students whose fiction discussed that day exhibits the most delicious, perception-altering use of language. Sometimes if they return for a second course with me, I give them writing exercises of my own invention and seventeen selected from *Copy and Compose* by Winston Weathers and Otis Winchester (1969), a splendid book that makes them compose new sentences in numerous forms: elaborated, compound/complex sentences; antithesis; various forms of key-word repetition; epanalepsis (circular sentence); and so forth.

This approach to teaching fiction-writing has been rewarding for my students and me. Occasionally, five or six of the best pupils continue on their own, meeting at one another's homes to discuss their stories. Former students have gone on to become successful novelists, college professors, editors, filmmakers, and even one Seattle detective who specializes in apprehending sexual offenders. (He told me that the class's emphasis on exactitude in language helps him write accurate police reports precise in their diction, thereby reducing the chances of a perpetrator going free because of foggy wording.) Another of my former students from the 1970s is Richard Gelfond, co-owner of IMAX, the big screen company, who received a special Academy Award for his contribution to our film experience.

However, that doesn't mean that over the last three decades I haven't been forced to modify this class, as the backgrounds and academic preparation of students and the enveloping culture have transmogrified. At some point in the late '80s, I realized that students were far less informed about the novels of depth and density I sometimes referred to (such as William Gaddis's *The Recognitions*, Thomas Mann's *Doctor Faustus*, and the aesthetic texts — Aristotle's *Poetics*, Longinus's essential *On the Sublime*, E. M. Forster's *Aspects of the Novel*, T. S. Eliot's "Tradition and the Individual Talent," Albert Murray's remarkable "The Hero and the Blues," Sartre's *What Is Literature?*, William Gass's "The Ontology of the Sentence, or How to Make a World of Words") — with which my better students in the '70s were at least glancingly familiar. In the period of identity politics and *Kulturkampf* that swept over American colleges in the '80s like a tsunami, students' imaginations cratered; their stories became depressingly less imaginative and daring, but more politically correct. Furthermore, I began to notice that some students timidly waited for me to analyze and dissect the fiction we were discussing that day or let a handful of the more vocal class members dominate our discussions. That, of course, would never do. This class was demanding, yes. They worked hard for their professor and themselves. But what I needed to ensure was that they worked just as hard for one another.

About ten years ago, I added a new task to the standard requirement that students provide hard copies of their fiction for all class members to edit. At the start of each discussion, one class member provides a full critique of whatever story is under review, and when he or she is done the rest of us offer our judgment of that story and the accuracy of the critic's analysis. Each student must perform this chore twice during a term, making it impossible for anyone to hide or withhold his or her judgment. I ask undergraduates to speak for at least ten minutes and graduate students for between twenty and forty-five minutes. If they identify a problem in the story under discussion, I ask them to suggest at least one—even better, two—solutions the author might try. Everyone in class needs to be prepared to step up and volunteer to take the place of that day's reporters if for some reason they miss class.

Because most students lack the critical skills for interrogating fiction (at first they even struggle with determining a story's literal sequence of events), I created for them a new handout, a checklist of twenty-four crucial questions they should ask in regard to fiction, not merely in terms of "themes" but about how a document is made, the decisions that went into its construction, and whether those were the best choices for fulfilling the writer's intention. After the student critique and our roundtable discussion, if time permits, the student critic and I lead a word-by-word analysis of the work, always with an eye toward explaining the principle of craft behind a correction or line that we praise.

To emphasize the importance of storytelling in addition to craft, I ask that every student turn in a complete, two-page plot outline for a new story each week. I want to nudge them beyond writing the same semiautobiographical story over and over, to imagine other lives, and to be raconteurs always ready to tell an engaging tale. Students generate ten outlines each term, enough to carry them into future workshops. For my graduate students, five of those have specific requisites: (1) one outline must use a classic reversal; (2) one must be in a traditional or neglected literary form not used for a major work of fiction in the last hundred years, a form students must go to the library and research; (3) one must use a historical figure, living or dead, as a protagonist or secondary character; (4) one must address some question, problem, or theme that hasn't been dramatized in contemporary American fiction; and (5) one must blend two or more traditional or contemporary forms of fiction. Many graduate students have told me that those weekly plot outlines were precisely what they needed to make them work on their greatest weaknesses: plot and dramatic structure.

Over nearly three decades, what I've discovered is that a writing workshop, like everything else, must evolve. If it is to truly help apprentice writers, it must deliver *techne*, what Gardner once called a deep understanding of "poetic and prosaic form, entertainment, and the powerful evocation of character and event." To internalize that understanding, I tell my students, serious writers must be edacious readers their entire lives. Yet, in the end, the galaxy of techniques and strategies we teachers provide our students—all that theory and practice—must serve spirited, memorable storytelling. It is toward that end that I've shaped, and continue to shape, this rather uncommon course on the craft of fiction.

8. Words

Language is the archives of history.
—Ralph Waldo Emerson

In all likelihood, the question of word choice haunts every serious apprentice writer. It certainly haunted me when I was in my late teens and early twenties, reading books on how to improve one's vocabulary and flagging words in books, magazine articles, news stories, and so forth that I didn't know. But that approach to improving one's word power, sad to say, is haphazard. And, as we all know, words are the most fundamental tool a writer has at his or her disposal. Sartre once wrote, "Every sentence is a risk." Well might he have added, "Every word is a risk," for precision in word choice is of paramount importance. In general, Americans use about twenty thousand words in their everyday discourse. But we know and recognize far more of the more than one million words in the English language. Scholars who have devoted themselves to this arcane research, and keep track of this sort of thing, report that Victor Hugo used fifteen thousand different words in his works, Shakespeare twelve thousand, and John Milton nine thousand. I recall once reading a provocative, challenging statement that said in the nineteenth century scholars typically read new editions of a dictionary to determine what new words had been officially added to the language, and which ones had fallen by the wayside. And Malcolm X passed his time in prison reading the dictionary. These matters kept tugging at me until in 1973 they reached a tipping point.

I was at dinner one evening at the farmhouse of John and Joan Gardner in southern Illinois. I made a comment about how much I was enjoying the poetic and archaic words John had used in his book-length epic poem, *Jason and Medeia*, many of which I had not encountered before. Joan replied that those words were there because she'd teased John about not having enough "big words" in his books, and John, with his magnifying glass in hand, went through every word in *The Compact Edition of the Oxford English Dictionary* before revising his update of the classic story. We had a good laugh about this, but her anecdote haunted me for days. I thought that if so many writers and scholars had gone to such trouble in being systematic about their word study, and now JG, too, then what was *my* excuse?

So the next year, when I was in the doctoral program in philosophy at Stony Brook, I did the same with *Webster's New Twentieth Century Dictionary*, which was a Christmas gift from my parents. It took me five months to plough through it, page after page for an hour every evening, night after night, as I developed for my own use a personal lexicon tailored specifically to my particular needs as a writer.

All that was long ago, but I've often wanted to repeat this exercise. What a lover of words and their beauty discovers after doing this chore (which soon ceases to be a chore and becomes a fascinating meditation on etymology, and on life itself in all its permutations) is that there is literally a word for *every* object, material or immaterial, every relation, and every process that human beings have experienced. Because that is what words are: the crystallization in language of thousands of years of experience across numerous cultures and civilizations, each word being the almost tangible flesh in which thought is tabernacled. To quote Sartre again: "The word *is* the Other," for it embodies the full spectrum of experiences, sensations, thoughts, and feelings in all their kaleidoscopic shades and hues that our species has lived through and recorded. The dictionary is our frabjous transcript for all of that (to borrow a word coined by Lewis Carroll to mean fabulous and delicious).

When writing, we will never, of course, deploy all the words we've learned. But a writer with an expansive vocabulary is much like a visual artist with many colors at his command. Regardless of the painting he's working on, he will always have the right colors available when he needs them. So, too, with a large vocabulary, you develop a sensitivity or feel, *Sprachgefühl*, for the exactly correct word for a thought or experience.

For that reason, my study is filled with dictionaries. The *Oxford* (with its included magnifying glass), of course. Seven dictionaries for Sanskrit, and two for Pali. One for French (my required graduate school language), and one for German. And nineteen others devoted to scrumptious poetic and archaic words, to British English, famous quotations, slang, American and world literature, Latin quotes, Indian philosophy, foreign words in general, terms for building and architecture, on the Bible (my wife has her own separate, well-stocked library of reference material on that subject), and other subjects. As with my *Webster's* in 1973, I've often sat down and gone through every page of some of these dictionaries (lately, the ones for Sanskrit), taking notes for building vocabulary. (For Sanskrit I have stacks of flash cards in Devanagari script for quick review.) In my experience there simply has been no other way to methodically and thoroughly acquire the general and technical words I require for the diverse subjects I'm called upon to write about.

9. In Defense of Our Language

Whenever I start reading something, the first thing I look for is a high level of language performance. It doesn't matter whether the work is fiction or nonfiction, if the prose is as pedestrian as the language we read in newspapers or overhear at the supermarket or DMV, merely utilitarian, then I will be disappointed and feel that the work is minimalistic. (And what passes for political discourse in this country—as well as the jargon of the Academy—is offensive enough to the ear and mind to make a lover of language run screaming from the room.) A literary work is, first and foremost, a performance of language. For that reason, I expect the instruments of expression—sentences and paragraphs—to be music and poetry. I expect them to be polished, and the writer to have at his or her command a mastery of the English tongue so complete and sophisticated that, as I read, I learn more about the possibilities of language performance. I want to be surprised by the prose, ambushed by its beauty. Words are the flesh of thought. And that means the language is my portal into the consciousness of the writer, who, on the page, is singing an interpretation of being that transforms and refines my reflections.

Language is sound and, therefore, is never "neutral." The sounds we make in speech are guttural, palatal, cerebral, dental, or labial. In *The Anatomy of Poetry* (1953), Marjorie Boulton makes it evident that on the level of what Aristotle once called *melos*, even the most microscopic datum of speech carries an affective quality or tone, and is sedimented with feeling or sense (and therefore not "neutral"). *B* and *p* sounds feel explosive; *m*, *n*, and *ng* we experience as humming and musical; *l* as liquescent, holding within itself something of streams, water, rest; *k*, *g*, *st*, *ts*, and *ch* are experienced as harsh; *t* and *d* are best suited for short actions; and *th* tends to be soothing. Emotion has *become* sound.

Our humanness, and especially our ability to achieve an intersubjective relationship with others in the social world, is based on the possibilities of language. In her essay "Philosophical Sketches," Susanne K. Langer eloquently captures this fact in a reiterated topic paragraph (to repeatedly drive home her topic) praised by Weathers and Winchester in *Copy and Compose* as being the very model for "first-class formal expository prose":

> Language, of course, is our prime instrument of conceptual expression. The things we say are in effect the things we can think. Words are the terms of our thinking as well as the terms in which we present our thoughts, because they present the objects of thought to the thinker himself. Before language communicates ideas, it gives them form, makes them clear, and in fact makes them what they are. Whatever has a name is an object of thought. Without words, sense experience is only a flow of impressions, as subjective as our feelings; words make it objective, and carve it up into *things* and *facts* that we can note, remember, and think about. Language gives outward experience its form and makes it definite and clear.

To a degree, then, I believe the health of a culture can be measured by the performance of those who speak and write its language. If that thesis is credible, then perhaps we should be worried by the coarseness, vulgarity, and at times obscenity that we encounter so often today in American speech. Something I've never forgotten about the community I grew up in is that I never heard adults swear. In all the decades I knew and closely observed him, my father never used an oath stronger than "Shoot!" when something bothered or frustrated him. The problem, as I see it, with vulgarity is that it is unexpressive, a failure of language to reveal things in a fresh way. Rather than liberate our perception, vulgarity calcifies it. As an example, consider Donald Trump repeating the p-word that someone in the audience at one of his speeches used to describe one of his rivals during the presidential campaign. In addition to being sexist, that word told us nothing about his rival.

As a much younger writer, I did think about all this. And today, more than thirty years later, I brood daily about the debasement of American speech. (In the last few decades we have mainstreamed many four-letter words in our fiction, stand-up comedy routines, and daily speech.) In his posthumously published book, *The Art of Fiction* (1984), Gardner said this: "Pettiness, vulgarity, bad taste fall away from him (the serious writer) automatically, and when he reads bad writers he notices their lapses of taste at once. He sees that they dwell on things Shakespeare would not have dwelled on, at his best, not because Shakespeare failed to notice them but because he saw their triviality. (Except to examine new techniques, or because of personal friendship, no serious apprentice should ever study second-rate writers.)"

In a world that offers us the truncated language we find on Twitter, the anonymity of the Internet, and the triumph of hip-hop and gangster rap, does anyone ever talk anymore about *taste*? Is that old-fashioned now and corny? Have we become, as American men and women, too liberated and progressive for good taste in our daily and literary use of language?

10. Telling It Long
and Telling It Short

If I don't control myself, my sentences in literary fiction naturally tend to run long, with image and idea building upon image and idea, rolling and ribboning out, sometimes twisting and torquing dialectically, from thesis to antithesis, and spiced with colons and semicolons and parenthetical asides (such as this) until I simply can't pack any more into them. I've always seen the sentence and paragraph as units of energy to be released. So yes, I use long sentences for rhythm and music. I most certainly would always follow one with a short sentence. As I used to teach my students, the technique here is to take the simple sentence, then "complicate" (i.e., extend) the subject, the verb, then the object.

To be frank, I think the elegant, long sentence is a thing of beauty, a self-contained entity worthy of study all by itself. Consider this sentence by Dylan Thomas from *Quite Early One Morning*:

I was born in a large Welsh town at the beginning of the Great War—an ugly, lovely town (or so it was and is to me), crawling, sprawling by a long and splendid curving shore where truant boys and sandfield boys and old men from nowhere, beachcombed, idled and paddled, watched the dock-bound ships or the ships streaming away into wonder and India, magic and China, countries bright with oranges and loud with lions; threw stones into the sea for the barking outcast dogs; made castles and forts and harbours and race tracks in the sand; and on Saturday afternoons listened to the brass band, watched the Punch and Judy, or hung about on the fringes of the crowd to hear the fierce religious speakers who shouted at the sea, as though it were wicked and wrong to roll in and out like that, white-horsed and full of fishes.

In *Copy and Compose: A Guide to Prose Style* (Prentice-Hall, 1969), Winston Weathers and Otis Winchester say this about Thomas's "master sentence":

In this magnificent sentence, loose and long, constituting an entire paragraph, great use is made of details placed in various forms of the series. After the initial statement the sentence proceeds descriptively, using double adjectives in front of nouns—"ugly, lovely town"—and double participles after the noun—"crawling, sprawling"—along with many instances of balance—"so it was and is to me," "long and splendid," "idled and paddled," and "bright with oranges and loud with lions." Note also the four-part series used: "castles and forts and harbours and race tracks." In the sentence abundant use is also made of sound devices: alliteration—"wicked and wrong"—and rhyme—"crawling, sprawling." And you will note the terminal rhythm of the sentence, after the long sweep of clauses and phrases: "as though it were wicked and wrong to roll in and out like that, white-horsed and full of fishes," with "white-horsed" a repositioned adjective, acting as a brake on the rhythmical flow.

We find the same detail and description, the same careful layering that is the result of much revision, and the same attention to balanced construction in the following sentence from Samuel Delany's *Flight from Nevèrÿon*:

No doubt in the palace his rough, if scarred good looks would cause (he dreamed) a few noble ladies to catch their breath; and perhaps even once, at some great party, into which he'd wandered only by accident, he'd exchange a few lines of banter with the Child Empress herself, whose reign is glittering and glorious, causing waves of jealousy and ire among the lords gathered at the affair, so that, after a month or so of such dalliance, his patroness (who by this time, would hopefully have taken up another lover, perhaps a young nobleman whose arrogant ways would make her fondly recall her nights and noons with him) would finally secure him an officer's commission in the Imperial Army, at some fascinating outpost in some exotic mountain hold, sending him on to who-knows-what great and gainful adventures . . .

No creative-writing student escaped my workshops for thirty-three years without doing as one of their many exercises sentences like the ones above. My hope is that each saw how the mastery of sentence forms was no less crucial for a writer than the mastery of larger units of literary construction.

11. Opening Sentences:
A Hundred Rays of Light

E. Ethelbert Miller asked me: "How important are first lines in novels?"

We know the answer to that question. First sentences of novels, chapters, or short stories are as crucial as final or concluding sentences. They are places of emphasis—just like the start and finish of the individual sentence. The editors at *American Book Review* once selected what they felt were the hundred best first lines for novels. I include this list for the reader's perusal and enjoyment with their permission.

	Quote	
1.	Call me Ishmael.	
2.	It is a truth universally acknowledged, that a single man in possession of a good fortune, must be in want of a wife.	
3.	A screaming comes across the sky.	
4.	Many years later, as he faced the firing squad, Colonel Aureliano Buendía was to remember that distant afternoon when his father took him to discover ice.	
5.	Lolita, light of my life, fire of my loins.	
6.	Happy families are all alike; every unhappy family is unhappy in its own way.	
7.	riverrun, past Eve and Adam's, from swerve of shore to bend of bay, brings us by a commodius vicus of recirculation back to Howth Castle and Environs.	
8.	It was a bright cold day in April, and the clocks were striking thirteen.	
9.	It was the best of times, it was the worst of times, it was the age of wisdom, it was the age of foolishness, it was the epoch of belief, it was the epoch of incredulity, it was the season of Light, it was the season of Darkness, it was the spring of hope, it was the winter of despair.	
10.	I am an invisible man.	
11.	The Miss Lonelyhearts of the New York *Post-Dispatch* (Are you in trouble?—Do-you-need-advice?—Write-to-Miss-Lonelyhearts-and-she-will-help-you) sat at his desk and stared at a piece of white cardboard.	
12.	You don't know about me without you have read a book by the name of *The Adventures of Tom Sawyer*; but that ain't no matter.	

Author	Title	Year
Herman Melville	*Moby-Dick*	1851
Jane Austen	*Pride and Prejudice*	1813
Thomas Pynchon	*Gravity's Rainbow*	1973
Gabriel García Márquez (trans. Gregory Rabassa)	*One Hundred Years of Solitude*	1967
Vladimir Nabokov	*Lolita*	1955
Leo Tolstoy (trans. Constance Garnett)	*Anna Karenina*	1877
James Joyce	*Finnegans Wake*	1939
George Orwell	*1984*	1949
Charles Dickens	*A Tale of Two Cities*	1859
Ralph Ellison	*Invisible Man*	1952
Nathanael West	*Miss Lonelyhearts*	1933
Mark Twain	*The Adventures of Huckleberry Finn*	1885

	Quote	
13.	Someone must have slandered Josef K., for one morning, without having done anything truly wrong, he was arrested.	
14.	You are about to begin reading Italo Calvino's new novel, *If on a winter's night a traveler.*	
15.	The sun shone, having no alternative, on the nothing new.	
16.	If you really want to hear about it, the first thing you'll probably want to know is where I was born, and what my lousy childhood was like, and how my parents were occupied and all before they had me, and all that David Copperfield kind of crap, but I don't feel like going into it, if you want to know the truth.	
17.	Once upon a time and a very good time it was there was a moocow coming down along the road and this moocow that was coming down along the road met a nicens little boy named baby tuckoo.	
18.	This is the saddest story I have ever heard.	
19.	I wish either my father or my mother, or indeed both of them, as they were in duty both equally bound to it, had minded what they were about when they begot me; had they duly considered how much depended upon what they were then doing;—that not only the production of a rational Being was concerned in it, but that possibly the happy formation and temperature of his body, perhaps his genius and the very cast of his mind;—and, for aught they knew to the contrary, even the fortunes of his whole house might take their turn from the humours and dispositions which were then uppermost:—Had they duly weighed and considered all this, and proceeded accordingly,—I am verily persuaded I should have made a quite different figure in the world, from that, in which the reader is likely to see me.	

Author	Title	Year
Franz Kafka (trans. Breon Mitchell)	*The Trial*	1925
Italo Calvino (trans. William Weaver)	*If on a winter's night a traveler*	1979
Samuel Beckett	*Murphy*	1938
J. D. Salinger	*The Catcher in the Rye*	1951
James Joyce	*A Portrait of the Artist as a Young Man*	1916
Ford Madox Ford	*The Good Soldier*	1915
Laurence Sterne	*Tristram Shandy*	1759–1767

	Quote	
20.	Whether I shall turn out to be the hero of my own life, or whether that station will be held by anybody else, these pages must show.	
21.	Stately, plump Buck Mulligan came from the stairhead, bearing a bowl of lather on which a mirror and a razor lay crossed.	
22.	It was a dark and stormy night; the rain fell in torrents, except at occasional intervals, when it was checked by a violent gust of wind which swept up the streets (for it is in London that our scene lies), rattling along the house-tops, and fiercely agitating the scanty flame of the lamps that struggled against the darkness.	
23.	One summer afternoon Mrs. Oedipa Maas came home from a Tupperware party whose hostess had put perhaps too much kirsch in the fondue to find that she, Oedipa, had been named executor, or she supposed executrix, of the estate of one Pierce Inverarity, a California real estate mogul who had once lost two million dollars in his spare time but still had assets numerous and tangled enough to make the job of sorting it all out more than honorary.	
24.	It was a wrong number that started it, the telephone ringing three times in the dead of night, and the voice on the other end asking for someone he was not.	
25.	Through the fence, between the curling flower spaces, I could see them hitting.	
26.	124 was spiteful.	
27.	Somewhere in la Mancha, in a place whose name I do not care to remember, a gentleman lived not long ago, one of those who has a lance and ancient shield on a shelf and keeps a skinny nag and a greyhound for racing.	

Author	Title	Year
Charles Dickens	*David Copperfield*	1850
James Joyce	*Ulysses*	1922
Edward George Bulwer-Lytton	*Paul Clifford*	1830
Thomas Pynchon	*The Crying of Lot 49*	1965
Paul Auster	*City of Glass*	1985
William Faulkner	*The Sound and the Fury*	1929
Toni Morrison	*Beloved*	1987
Miguel de Cervantes (trans. Edith Grossman)	*Don Quixote*	1605

	Quote	
28.	Mother died today.	
29.	Every summer Lin Kong returned to Goose Village to divorce his wife, Shuyu.	
30.	The sky above the port was the color of television, tuned to a dead channel.	
31.	I am a sick man . . . I am a spiteful man.	
32.	Where now? Who now? When now?	
33.	Once an angry man dragged his father along the ground through his own orchard. "Stop!" cried the groaning old man at last, "Stop! I did not drag my father beyond this tree."	
34.	In a sense, I am Jacob Horner.	
35.	It was like so, but wasn't.	
36.	—Money . . . in a voice that rustled.	
37.	Mrs. Dalloway said she would buy the flowers herself.	
38.	All this happened, more or less.	
39.	They shoot the white girl first.	
40.	For a long time, I went to bed early.	
41.	The moment one learns English, complications set in.	
42.	Dr. Weiss, at forty, knew that her life had been ruined by literature.	
43.	I was the shadow of the waxwing slain / By the false azure in the windowpane;	

Author	Title	Year
Albert Camus (trans. Stuart Gilbert)	*The Stranger*	1942
Ha Jin	*Waiting*	1999
William Gibson	*Neuromancer*	1984
Fyodor Dostoyevsky (trans. Michael R. Katz)	*Notes from Underground*	1864
Samuel Beckett (trans. Patrick Bowles)	*The Unnamable*	1953
Gertrude Stein	*The Making of Americans*	1925
John Barth	*The End of the Road*	1958
Richard Powers	*Galatea 2.2*	1995
William Gaddis	*J R*	1975
Virginia Woolf	*Mrs. Dalloway*	1925
Kurt Vonnegut	*Slaughterhouse-Five*	1969
Toni Morrison	*Paradise*	1998
Marcel Proust (trans. Lydia Davis)	*Swann's Way*	1913
Felipe Alfau	*Chromos*	1990
Anita Brookner	*The Debut*	1981
Vladimir Nabokov	*Pale Fire*	1962

	Quote	
44.	Ships at a distance have every man's wish on board.	
45.	I had the story, bit by bit, from various people, and, as generally happens in such cases, each time it was a different story.	
46.	Ages ago, Alex, Allen and Alva arrived at Antibes, and Alva allowing all, allowing anyone, against Alex's admonition, against Allen's angry assertion: another African amusement . . . anyhow, as all argued, an awesome African army assembled and arduously advanced against an African anthill, assiduously annihilating ant after ant, and afterward, Alex astonishingly accuses Albert as also accepting Africa's antipodal ant annexation.	
47.	There was a boy called Eustace Clarence Scrubb, and he almost deserved it.	
48.	He was an old man who fished alone in a skiff in the Gulf Stream and he had gone eighty-four days now without taking a fish.	
49.	It was the day my grandmother exploded.	
50.	I was born twice: first, as a baby girl, on a remarkably smogless Detroit day in January of 1960; and then again, as a teenage boy, in an emergency room near Petoskey, Michigan, in August of 1974.	
51.	Elmer Gantry was drunk.	
52.	We started dying before the snow, and like the snow, we continued to fall.	
53.	It was a pleasure to burn.	
54.	A story has no beginning or end; arbitrarily one chooses that moment of experience from which to look back or from which to look ahead.	

Author	Title	Year
Zora Neale Hurston	*Their Eyes Were Watching God*	1937
Edith Wharton	*Ethan Frome*	1911
Walter Abish	*Alphabetical Africa*	1974
C. S. Lewis	*The Voyage of the Dawn Treader*	1952
Ernest Hemingway	*The Old Man and the Sea*	1952
Iain Banks	*The Crow Road*	1992
Jeffrey Eugenides	*Middlesex*	2002
Sinclair Lewis	*Elmer Gantry*	1927
Louise Erdrich	*Tracks*	1988
Ray Bradbury	*Fahrenheit 451*	1953
Graham Greene	*The End of the Affair*	1951

	Quote	
55.	Having placed in my mouth sufficient bread for three minutes' chewing, I withdrew my powers of sensual perception and retired into the privacy of my mind, my eyes and face assuming a vacant and preoccupied expression.	
56.	I was born in the Year 1632, in the City of York, of a good Family, tho' not of that Country, my Father being a Foreigner of Bremen, who settled first at *Hull*; He got a good Estate by Merchandise, and leaving off his Trade, lived afterward at *York*, from whence he had married my Mother, whose Relations were named Robinson, a very good Family in that Country, and from whom I was called Robinson Kreutznaer; but by the usual Corruption of Words in England, we are now called, nay we call our selves, and write our Name Crusoe, and so my Companions always call'd me.	
57.	In the beginning, sometimes I left messages in the street.	
58.	Miss Brooke had that kind of beauty which seems to be thrown into relief by poor dress.	
59.	It was love at first sight.	
60.	What if this young woman, who writes such bad poems, in competition with her husband, whose poems are equally bad, should stretch her remarkably long and well-made legs out before you, so that her skirt slips up to the tops of her stockings?	
61.	I have never begun a novel with more misgiving.	
62.	Once upon a time, there was a woman who discovered she had turned into the wrong person.	
63.	The human race, to which so many of my readers belong, has been playing at children's games from the beginning, and will probably do it till the end, which is a nuisance for the few people who grow up.	

Author	Title	Year
Flann O'Brien	*At Swim-Two-Birds*	1939
Daniel Defoe	*Robinson Crusoe*	1719
David Markson	*Wittgenstein's Mistress*	1988
George Eliot	*Middlemarch*	1872
Joseph Heller	*Catch-22*	1961
Gilbert Sorrentino	*Imaginative Qualities of Actual Things*	1971
W. Somerset Maugham	*The Razor's Edge*	1944
Anne Tyler	*Back When We Were Grownups*	2001
G. K. Chesterton	*The Napoleon of Notting Hill*	1904

	Quote	
64.	In my younger and more vulnerable years my father gave me some advice that I've been turning over in my mind ever since.	
65.	You better not never tell nobody but God.	
66.	"To be born again," sang Gibreel Farishta tumbling from the heavens, "first you have to die."	
67.	It was a queer, sultry summer, the summer they electrocuted the Rosenbergs, and I didn't know what I was doing in New York.	
68.	Most really pretty girls have pretty ugly feet, and so does Mindy Metalman, Lenore notices, all of a sudden.	
69.	If I am out of my mind, it's all right with me, thought Moses Herzog.	
70.	Francis Marion Tarwater's uncle had been dead for only half a day when the boy got too drunk to finish digging his grave and a Negro named Buford Munson, who had come to get a jug filled, had to finish it and drag the body from the breakfast table where it was still sitting and bury it in a decent and Christian way, with the sign of its Saviour at the head of the grave and enough dirt on top to keep the dogs from digging it up.	
71.	Granted: I am an inmate of a mental hospital; my keeper is watching me, he never lets me out of his sight; there's a peephole in the door, and my keeper's eye is the shade of brown that can never see through a blue-eyed type like me.	
72.	When Dick Gibson was a little boy he was not Dick Gibson.	
73.	Hiram Clegg, together with his wife Emma and four friends of the faith from Randolph Junction, were summoned by the Spirit and Mrs. Clara Collins, widow of the beloved Nazarene preacher Ely Collins, to West Condon on the weekend of the eighteenth and nineteenth of April, there to await the End of the World.	

Author	Title	Year
F. Scott Fitzgerald	*The Great Gatsby*	1925
Alice Walker	*The Color Purple*	1982
Salman Rushdie	*The Satanic Verses*	1988
Sylvia Plath	*The Bell Jar*	1963
David Foster Wallace	*The Broom of the System*	1987
Saul Bellow	*Herzog*	1964
Flannery O'Connor	*The Violent Bear It Away*	1960
Gunter Grass (trans. Ralph Manheim)	*The Tin Drum*	1959
Stanley Elkin	*The Dick Gibson Show*	1971
Robert Coover	*The Origin of the Brunists*	1966

	Quote	
74.	She waited, Kate Croy, for her father to come in, but he kept her unconscionably, and there were moments at which she showed herself, in the glass over the mantel, a face positively pale with the irritation that had brought her to the point of going away without sight of him.	
75.	In the late summer of that year we lived in a house in a village that looked across the river and the plain to the mountains.	
76.	"Take my camel, dear," said my Aunt Dot, as she climbed down from this animal on her return from High Mass.	
77.	He was an inch, perhaps two, under six feet, powerfully built, and he advanced straight at you with a slight stoop of the shoulders, head forward, and a fixed from-under stare which made you think of a charging bull.	
78.	The past is a foreign country; they do things differently there.	
79.	On my naming day when I come 12 I gone front spear and kilt a wyld boar he parbly ben the las wyld pig on the Bundel Downs any how there hadnt ben none for a long time befor him nor I aint looking to see none agen.	
80.	Justice?—You get justice in the next world, in this world you have the law.	
81.	Vaughan died yesterday in his last car-crash.	
82.	I write this sitting in the kitchen sink.	
83.	"When your mama was the geek, my dreamlets," Papa would say, "she made the nipping off of noggins such a crystal mystery that the hens themselves yearned toward her, waltzing around her, hypnotized with longing."	

Author	Title	Year
Henry James	*The Wings of the Dove*	1902
Ernest Hemingway	*A Farewell to Arms*	1929
Rose Macaulay	*The Towers of Trebizond*	1956
Joseph Conrad	*Lord Jim*	1900
L. P. Hartley	*The Go-Between*	1953
Russell Hoban	*Riddley Walker*	1980
William Gaddis	*A Frolic of His Own*	1994
J. G. Ballard	*Crash*	1973
Dodie Smith	*I Capture the Castle*	1948
Katherine Dunn	*Geek Love*	1983

	Quote	
84.	In the last years of the seventeenth century there was to be found among the fops and fools of the London coffee-houses one rangy, gangling flitch called Ebenezer Cooke, more ambitious than talented, and yet more talented than prudent, who, like his friends-in-folly, all of whom were supposed to be educating at Oxford or Cambridge, had found the sound of Mother English more fun to game with than her sense to labor over, and so rather than applying himself to the pains of scholarship, had learned the knack of versifying, and ground out quires of couplets after the fashion of the day, afroth with Joves and Jupiters, aclang with jarring rhymes, and string-taut with similes stretched to the snapping-point.	
85.	When I finally caught up with Abraham Trahearne, he was drinking beer with an alcoholic bulldog named Fireball Roberts in a ramshackle joint just outside of Sonoma, California, drinking the heart right out of a fine spring afternoon.	
86.	It was just noon that Sunday morning when the sheriff reached the jail with Lucas Beauchamp though the whole town (the whole county too for that matter) had known since the night before that Lucas had killed a white man.	
87.	I, Tiberius Claudius Drusus Nero Germanicus This-that-and-the-other (for I shall not trouble you yet with all my titles) who was once, and not so long ago either, known to my friends and relatives and associates as "Claudius the Idiot," or "That Claudius," or "Claudius the Stammerer," or "Clau-Clau-Claudius" or at best as "Poor Uncle Claudius," am now about to write this strange history of my life; starting from my earliest childhood and continuing year by year until I reach the fateful point of change where, (cont.)	

Author	Title	Year
John Barth	*The Sot-Weed Factor*	1960
James Crumley	*The Last Good Kiss*	1978
William Faulkner	*Intruder in the Dust*	1948
Robert Graves	*I, Claudius*	1934

	Quote	
	some eight years ago, at the age of fifty-one, I suddenly found myself caught in what I may call the "golden predicament" from which I have never since become disentangled.	
88.	Of all the things that drive men to sea, the most common disaster, I've come to learn, is women.	
89.	I am an American, Chicago born—Chicago, that somber city—and go at things as I have taught myself, free-style, and will make the record in my own way: first to knock, first admitted; sometimes an innocent knock, sometimes a not so innocent.	
90.	The towers of Zenith aspired above the morning mist; austere towers of steel and cement and limestone, sturdy as cliffs and delicate as silver rods.	
91.	I will tell you in a few words who I am: lover of the hummingbird that darts to the flower beyond the rotted sill where my feet are propped; lover of bright needlepoint and the bright stitching fingers of humorless old ladies bent to their sweet and infamous designs; lover of parasols made from the same puffy stuff as a young girl's underdrawers; still lover of that small naval boat which somehow survived the distressing years of my life between her decks or in her pilothouse; and also lover of poor dear black Sonny, my mess boy, fellow victim and confidant, and of my wife and child. But most of all, lover of my harmless and sanguine self.	
92.	He was born with a gift of laughter and a sense that the world was mad.	
93.	Psychics can see the color of time it's blue.	
94.	In the town, there were two mutes and they were always together.	

Author	Title	Year
Charles Johnson	*Middle Passage*	1990
Saul Bellow	*The Adventures of Augie March*	1953
Sinclair Lewis	*Babbitt*	1922
John Hawkes	*Second Skin*	1964
Rafael Sabatini	*Scaramouche*	1921
Ronald Sukenick	*Blown Away*	1986
Carson McCullers	*The Heart Is a Lonely Hunter*	1940

	Quote	
95.	Once upon a time two or three weeks ago, a rather stubborn and determined middle-aged man decided to record for posterity, exactly as it happened, word by word and step by step, the story of another man for indeed what is great in man is that he is a bridge and not a goal, a somewhat paranoiac fellow unmarried, unattached, and quite irresponsible, who had decided to lock himself in a room a furnished room with a private bath, cooking facilities, a bed, a table, and at least one chair, in New York City, for a year 365 days to be precise, to write the story of another person—a shy young man about of [sic] 19 years old—who, after the war the Second World War, had come to America the land of opportunities from France under the sponsorship of his uncle—a journalist, fluent in five languages—who himself had come to America from Europe Poland it seems, though this was not clearly established sometime during the war after a series of rather gruesome adventures, and who, at the end of the war, wrote to the father his cousin by marriage of the young man whom he considered as a nephew, curious to know if he the father and his family had survived the German occupation, and indeed was deeply saddened to learn, in a letter from the young man—a long and touching letter written in English, not by the young man, however, who did not know a damn word of English, but by a good friend of his who had studied English in school—that his parents both his father and mother and his two sisters one older and the other younger than he had been deported they were Jewish to a German concentration camp Auschwitz probably and never returned, no doubt having been exterminated deliberately X * X * X * X, and that, therefore, the young man who was now an orphan, a displaced person, who, during the war, (*cont.*)	

Author	Title	Year
Raymond Federman	*Double or Nothing*	1971

	Quote	
	had managed to escape deportation by working very hard on a farm in Southern France, would be happy and grateful to be given the opportunity to come to America that great country he had heard so much about and yet knew so little about to start a new life, possibly go to school, learn a trade, and become a good, loyal citizen.	
96.	Time is not a line but a dimension, like the dimensions of space.	
97.	He—for there could be no doubt of his sex, though the fashion of the time did something to disguise it— was in the act of slicing at the head of a Moor which swung from the rafters.	
98.	High, high above the North Pole, on the first day of 1969, two professors of English Literature approached each other at a combined velocity of 1200 miles per hour.	
99.	They say when trouble comes close ranks, and so the white people did.	
100.	The cold passed reluctantly from the earth, and the retiring fogs revealed an army stretched out on the hills, resting.	

Author	Title	Year
Margaret Atwood	*Cat's Eye*	1988
Virginia Woolf	*Orlando*	1928
David Lodge	*Changing Places*	1975
Jean Rhys	*Wide Sargasso Sea*	1966
Stephen Crane	*The Red Badge of Courage*	1895

12. On Craft and Revision

In fiction there must be a theoretical basis to the most minute details. Even a single glove must have its theory.
—Prosper Mérimée

It is in self-limitation that a master first shows himself.
—Goethe

A classic is a book that doesn't have to be written again.
—Carl Van Doren

The late John Gardner, my writing mentor more than thirty years ago, once told a story about revision that has stuck with me. He said he gave a reading, and during the Q&A a woman raised her hand and said, "You know, I think I like your writing, but I don't think I like *you*." His reply was memorable. "That's all right," he said, "because I'm a better person when I'm writing. Standing here, talking to you now, I can't revise my words. If I say something wrong or not quite right, or maybe offensive and it hurts someone, the words are out there, public, and I can't take them back. I have to rely on you to revise or fix them for me. But when I'm writing, I can go over and over what I think and say until it's right."

I think Gardner captured the heart of the creative process.

We often hear that 90 percent of good writing is rewriting. We also know that writing well is the same thing as thinking well, and that means we want our final literary product—story, novel, or essay—to exhibit our best thought, best feeling, and best technique.

When I compose a first draft I just let everything I feel and think spill out raw and chaotically on the page. I let it be a mess. I trust my instincts. I just let my ideas and feelings flow until I run out of words. It's fine for an early draft to be a disaster area. I don't censor myself. When I have this raw copy, I can then decide if this idea is worth putting more effort into. If so, then with the second draft, I clean up spelling and grammar. I add anything I forgot to include in the first draft and take out whatever isn't working.

Then the real fun begins with the third draft. (Despite its importance, art should always be a form of play.) That's where I work on what I know are my creative weaknesses. There are many, but let me focus on just one—poetic description, achieving what Gerard Manley Hopkins called *inscape*, and a granularity of specifics and detail. As a cartoonist and illustrator, I think visually first. Like most writers, my images overwhelmingly represent *sight*, what I see. We do have a built-in bias for visual imagery. We say we "see" (or hear) the truth. Never do we say we touch or feel it. So, in that third draft, I work consciously to include whenever possible imagery for the other senses—taste, smell, touch. If need be, I'll resort to synaesthesia, or describing the experience of one of our senses using the language of another. Or onomatopoeia. With taste and smell, for example, my goal would be to describe odor as well as Upton Sinclair did in the "Stockyards" section of *The Jungle*; and sound as well as Lafcadio Hearn handles it. A book in my library that helped me much with this when I first started writing was *The Art of Description* by Marjorie H. Nicolson (New York: F. S. Crofts & Co., 1928).

Another problem I often have, personally, is at the idea stage. I sometimes start out with too many ideas. Before I begin to write, my thoughts are bursting with possibilities for the stories, multiple layers of meaning, things I'd love to include, all of which I jot down as quickly as they come to me. But then at some point I realize that less *is* more when one is plotting a story, if one wants it to be an economical, efficient, and coherent aesthetic object. Inevitably, I always have to scale things back, to search for and find the simple action and structure that creates suspense, causation that feels logical and inexorable, and a clean, uncluttered emotional through-line, i.e., what to emphasize and what to mute. With that decided, I then know how to place the discarded idea in a new way in the composition.

In that third draft, I begin to polish sentences and paragraphs for style. I always need a minimum of *three* drafts before I have anything worthy of showing to others, and that's only if I'm lucky. (Don't get me wrong: my drafts are not separate entities completed from start to finish. They flow into each other. I'm constantly rethinking a story's beginning as I work on the middle and end.) Sometimes my ratio of throwaway to keep pages is 20:1. From the third draft forward, I work at varying sentence length (long, short) in every paragraph, and also varying sentence forms (simple, compound, complex, loose, periodic). I see each sentence as being a unit of energy. The music and meaning of each sentence and paragraph must carry into the next and contribute to a larger rhythmic design.

I try to make sure each paragraph can justify its being on the page. That is, each paragraph should have at least *one* good idea in it. Or do *some*thing to advance the story. Or enrich the details of the world in which the story is taking place or the characterizations of its people. I work at being as artistically generous as possible. I work to amplify a strong narrative voice. I want intellectual and imagistic density. And I want to achieve, of course, the feeling of organic story flow. I rewrite and edit until the piece has no waste or unnecessary sentences whatsoever. Nothing that slows down the pace of the story. Any sentence that *can* come out *should* come out. ("Kill your babies," as the saying goes, unless, of course, you absolutely love that sentence.) There should be no *remplissage* (literary padding) or *longueur* (long and boring passages). No irrelevant postcard details in background descriptions. I want every detail to be "significant," i.e., revealing in terms of character, place, or event. I work to get music—rhythm, meter—between sentences and paragraphs, as if the prose composition is actually a musical work, one pleasing to the ear. The way to test this is to read it out loud. If I stumble when reading the piece, I know those sentences that tripped me up (that were hard to say or recite) need to be rewritten. Also, I try to be generous with concrete language, and to write always with specificity. (The Devil is always in the details.)

I try, as I rework and revise, to remember a note I made to myself in my writer's notebooks: "In great fiction the main element of importance is the fusion of *character* and *event*, their interplay, the way the latter reveals the former, and the way the former leads inevitably to the latter. One must also see how event transforms character even as it is produced by character."

Character, then, is the engine of plot, and over the years I've come at the creation of characters from a few different angles: (1) basing them on an idea or principle; (2) drawing them from real people, specific individuals (or several) as my model for a character; (3) basing them on myself; and (4) basing them on the biography of a historical figure. Quite often, my characters combine all those approaches.

So for me, revision is a combination of cutting away (like sculpting the sentence from stone) and also a constant layering of the language (like working with the sentence as you would clay). The palimpsestic layering part of the process often leads to sudden surprises — puns, oracles, and revelations — that I'm always looking for. And these discoveries often redirect the story away from my original idea or conception. Back and forth, adding and subtracting, like that. You know when a piece is finished, because you can't pull out a single sentence or change a word or syllable. If you do extract that heavily polished sentence, you create a hole in the space *between* the sentences before and after it, since you have altered not only the sense but the sound that links those sentences. (It's like ripping an arm off a human body, an act that affects everything else in the organism you're creating.) Achieving this requires (for me) lots of thrown-away pages: 1,200 for *Faith and the Good Thing*, 2,400 for *Oxherding Tale*, 3,000 for *Middle Passage*, and more than 3,000 for *Dreamer*. I use this same method for short stories. I guess I don't so much write stories as sculpt them. I love the sustained focus this requires, for it is so much like the first stage in formal meditation, called *dharana* (or concentration).

I started keeping a diary when I was twelve; my mother suggested the idea, mainly so she could read it and learn what feelings and secrets I was keeping from her. I remember her asking once at dinner, "Why don't you like your uncle So-and-so?" and I thought, Dang! She must be a mind reader, then I realized she'd been reading the diary, and from that point on I had to hide it from her. In college the diary transformed into a journal in which I wrote poetry and brief essays to myself, and (as with a diary) tried to make sense of daily events. (These old journals fill up one filing cabinet in my study.) When I started writing fiction, the journals moved in the direction of being a writing tool and memory aide.

I use cheap, unlined spiral notebooks, each page like a blank canvas. Into them go notes on literally *every*thing I experience or think worth remembering during the day; I jot down images, phrases used by my friends, fragments of thoughts, overheard dialogue, anything I flag in something I've read that strikes me for its sentence form or memorable qualities, its beauty or truth. These writing notebooks since 1972 sit on one of my bookshelves thirty inches deep, along with notebooks I kept from college classes. (I save everything; it's shameless.) After forty-three years of accumulation, the notebooks contain notes on just about every subject under the sun. When I have a decent third draft, I begin going carefully through my notebooks, page after page, hunting for thoughts, images I've had, or ideas about characters (observations I've made of people around me), carefully selecting from my notebooks details like someone arranging a Japanese rock garden. Although it can sometimes take five days (eight hours a day), and even two weeks, to go through all these notebooks and folders (since I add something new to the current one every day), I can always count on finding *some* sentence, phrase, or idea I had, say, twenty or thirty years ago that is perfect for a novel or story in progress. The literary journal *Zyzzyva* used to publish a feature called "The Writer's Notebook." If you look at the Fall 1992 issue (pages 124–43), you'll see reproductions of my revised pages and an early outline for *Middle Passage*, as well as character notes for Captain Ebenezer Falcon that I wrote on hotel stationery (the Sheraton-Palace Hotel in San Francisco) when I was on the road.

When I tell students the anecdote about Gardner, I emphasize his feeling that the result of this painstaking revision process is that for at least *once* in their lives, here on the page, they can achieve perfection or something close to that, if they are willing to revise and reenvision their work long enough. And then I say: Where else in life do we get the chance—the privilege and blessing—to lovingly, selflessly go over something again and again until it finally embodies exactly what we think and feel, our best expression, our vision at its clear-est, and our best *techne*?

Or, as Jeffery Allen said in an interview about his novel *Song of the Shank*, "I really tried hard to get it right. Art may be the only form of perfection available to humans, and creat-ing a work of art might be the only thing in life that we have full control over. So we might ask, How is great measured? Craft is certainly one thing. I would also like to think that certain works of art transform the artist."

13. The Challenge of Voice

*Style is never simply technical choice, but evolves from
how a writer sees the world. . . . [To embrace] a read-
ily identifiable prose style without being aware of its
tyranny and inevitability of voice . . . [is to embrace] a
ready-made point of view.*
— Linsey Abrams, "A Maximalist Novelist
Looks at Some Minimalist Fiction"

Best be yourself, imperial, plain and true.
— Elizabeth Barrett Browning

In the late 1960s when I was a journalism major, I had a professor who was fond of giving his students a copy of a decades-
old newspaper article, with the author's name removed, and
asking them to identify who wrote it. Just as art history students are tested on recognizing an anonymous painting, and
music students on naming a composer based on an uniden-
tified scrap of his music, so, too, this professor expected us
to determine the newspaperman who did this piece by its
style and voice alone. A couple of class members rose to the
occasion. (I was one of them, but only because I had a friend
who took this class before me and told me the answer.) The
piece in question was by Ernest Hemingway, who created a
major writing style. If you knew his fiction, you were certain

to recognize the personality and linguistic decisions in this newspaper story. For many readers and writers "voice" is a dimension of writing that proves to be elusive, intangible, and difficult to define. Often some people will just say, as they do of pornography, "I know it when I see it." But when we *don't* see it, which is usually the case with student fiction and much of published writing, we must judge that work of fiction to be *un*voiced or voice*less*, and therefore lacking in one of literature's more subtle and important dimensions. But, yes, this subject is difficult to discuss, for in order to do so we must talk about an artist's individual vision, his unique approach to language and viewpoint in fiction. Language precedes us. We find it "out there" in the social world, and we must learn its rules, its logic. In developing a voice what the writer does is transform or personalize the expressive instrument— language—adapting and individuating it to fit his experience, his vision of the world. Voice and vision, these are two sides of the same phenomenon. And I would venture to say voice is absent in apprentice writing precisely because the writer has yet to develop for himself (or herself) a vision of how the world works.

There are writers possessing a very strong temperament, and for them the specificity of their individual voices is one of the delights of their fiction, just as much as their stories (for their voices *are* the vehicles by which their stories are delivered with panache). For that reason they never change voice from one book to another. Just as with their speaking voice, their literary voice has its individual tics, quirks, and eccentricities. An example? At the moment I'm thinking of P. G. Wodehouse, Kurt Vonnegut, and perhaps I'll throw in D. H. Lawrence, too, but you can easily add other authors to this list. It's possible, even likely probable, that my nonfiction falls into this category, especially when I'm writing about Buddhism. But as a storyteller I tend to deliberately practice what some have called "narrative ventriloquism," or changing my voice to fit the story being told. Think of this as being like the way a puppet master switches voices for a Punch-and-Judy performance. Or, if you like, just think of it as putting on a mask for the duration of a fiction.

Changing voices is de rigueur for writing first-person stories, if the teller of the tale is not the author himself or herself. Every actor not just playing himself on stage is adept at this form of shape-shifting; the very ability to put on a mask is itself an indication that we do not have a static, unchanging, enduring "self" but instead the ontological condition of emptiness, or *shūnyatā*, as Buddhists say—would acting even be possible if the self was a *substance* or essentialist or an unchanging Parmenidean entity?—but we should leave that lecture for another time. Consider the opening—tone, diction, personality—of the nameless professor who opens my story "Alēthia":

> God willing, I'm going to tell you a love story. A skeptical old man, whose great forehead and gray forked beard most favor (when I flatter myself) those of that towering sociologist W. E. B. Du Bois, I am hardly a man to conjure a fabulation so odd in its transfiguration of things, so strange, so terrifying (thus it now seems to me) that it belongs on the pale lips of the poetic genius who wrote *Essentials* and that hallucinatory prose-poem called *Cane*.

Now compare that opening with the one for my story "Exchange Value," where the narrator is a teenager named Cooter living on Chicago's South Side:

> Me and my brother, Loftis, came in by the old lady's window. There was some kinda boobytrap—boxes

of broken glass—that shoulda warned us Miss Bailey wasn't the easy mark we made her to be.

Obviously, neither of these voices—one from the Academy, the other from the street—can be called *my* normal voice. Yet ironically, they briefly became my voice and temperament during the time of each fiction's composition. (Potentially, we all have *many* voices within us. Think for just a moment about the black scholar, a PhD, who can lecture on nanotechnology one moment, then cuss you out the next moment if you make the mistake of stepping on his shoes.) This is how first person in fiction operates. I should also point out something else. In a post dated September 6, 2011, entitled "One Minute Past Midnight," I mentioned that a minor character in my most recently written, third-person story speaks in Cockney slang. Were *he* to become the narrator for that story, then I, as a writer, would have to compose *every* sentence so that each becomes a window onto his unique world of experience.

All of the above should be obvious for when one writes in first person. But that same sense of voice and personality should resonate, I believe, in third-person narratives as well. In the tale-telling tradition, this is fairly easy to do, as in the opening for my story "The Sorcerer's Apprentice," for it employs a traditional and familiar stock voice:

> There a was time, long ago, when many sorcerers lived in South Carolina, men not long from slavery who remembered the white magic of the Ekpe Cults and Cameroons, and by far the greatest of these wizards was a blacksmith named Rubin Bailey.

But a third-person voice that isn't stock can also cling to every sentence—and word choice—as in my story "The Education of Mingo." The following example describes the farmer Moses Green's efforts to "educate" a slave named Mingo.

Now Moses Green was not a man for doing things half-way. Education, as he dimly understood it, was as serious as a heart attack. You had to have a model, a good Christian gentleman like Moses himself, to wash a Moor white in a single generation. As he taught Mingo farming and table etiquette, ciphering with knotted string, and how to cook ashcakes, Moses constantly revised himself. He tried not to cuss, although any mention of Martin Van Buren or Free-Soilers made his stomach chew itself; or sop cornbread in his coffee; or pick his nose at public market.

Here we have third-person narration *limited* to Moses Green. It is as if we as readers are perched on his shoulder, seeing everything from his point of view. And so the narration at times (or most times) is flavored with his speech patterns and diction, just as it would be in his dialogue.

14. How We Sound

Voice can be an elusive dimension in fiction, but it is an element of craft I've devoted myself to exploring since 1972. In his recent essay on "Popper's Disease," Tom Williams also touches upon other stories in that collection, *The Sorcerer's Apprentice*, and describes the tale "Exchange Value" as "a story in dialect . . . that rivals Hurston and Twain."

Obviously, the "dialect" Williams refers to in that story is nothing like the Negro dialect we associate with, say, the work of Paul Laurence Dunbar. Nor does it resemble the caricatured form of black speech we see in the Plantation school writers or, for that matter, in Mark Twain's black characters. In those cases, you will notice, all the black characters speak the same way in a kind of generic, butchered English that fails to individuate one black speaker from another. This is simply the wrong way—the lazy way—to put speech in the mouths of black characters, because like all human beings every black person speaks differently. Consider this observation by the philosopher R. G. Collingwood:

> Speech is after all only a system of gestures, having the peculiarity that each gesture produces a characteristic sound, so that it can be perceived through the ear as well as through the eye. Listening to a speaker instead of looking at him tends to make us think of speech as essentially a system of sounds; but it is not; essentially it is a

system of gestures made with the lungs and larynx, and the cavities of the mouth and nose. We get still farther away from the fundamental facts about speech when we think of it as something that can be written and read, forgetting that what writing, in our clumsy notations, can represent is only a small part of the spoken sound, where pitch and stress, tempo and rhythm, are almost entirely ignored. But even a writer or reader, unless the words are to fall flat or meaningless, must speak them soundlessly to himself. The written or printed book is only a series of hints, as elliptical as the neumes of Byzantine music, from which the reader thus works out for himself the speech-gestures which alone have the gift of expression.

As an exercise, think of how you might portray different cadences, intonations, accents, tempo, inflections, and speech-sound qualities in dialogue for Barack Obama, 50 Cent, Rev. Jeremy Wright, Louis Armstrong, Billie Holiday, or Ethel Waters. Is it possible to have something of their unique sound "cling" to the words we place on the page for them to speak? In other words, to *not* ignore, as Collingwood puts it, "pitch and stress, tempo and rhythm"? Personally, right now and whenever I think of the next story I wish to write, whether in first or third person, regardless of whether it is set in the past or the present, I'm intrigued by the idea of creating a character who primarily speaks in periodic sentences — like this one you just read.

When I wrote "Exchange Value" with the story in the voice of the character Cooter, my aim was to see if a philosophical fiction, one about our experience of money, could be the vehicle for a voice entirely rendered in contemporary (at the time, the late '70s) black slang. That language is 180 degrees different from the first-person narrator of "Popper's Disease," who is a physician acquainted with many sciences; and it differs yet again from the third-person narrative voice of the title story for the collection, which is the voice of the traditional folktale or fairy-tale storyteller. The first observation to make, then, is that there are potentially as many black narrative voices as there are black people—voices flavored with a West Indian patois, or ones that are black and British. None is more "authentic" than any other. Compare the voices of Frederick Douglass, Rev. Richard Allen, Phillis Wheatley, and the character Tiberius in the collection *Soulcatcher and Other Stories*. Each differs in diction based on their background, education, and the way each individually tailors language to his or her vision of the world. The ideal in a work of fiction would be for the dialogue for each character to be so unique and specific to him or her that we could dispense altogether with the tags "he said" and "she said," just as we don't need them to recognize people we know speaking around us in a room. For an example, see my story "Poetry and Politics," which is all dialogue without a single line of description or narration.

The second observation to make is that achieving narrative ventriloquism requires that (1) a writer must have an ear sensitive to the rich variety of black (and white and other) voices around him; (2) he or she must carefully weigh each possible word choice so that the voice is consistent; and (3) the writer, like an actor, must enjoy playing a role or putting on a mask for the duration of the story.

Ideally, a line by a first-person narrator in, for example, *Middle Passage* cannot be lifted from the text and simply dropped into *Dreamer*. In the former novel, Rutherford Calhoun's speech is textured by the language of sailors and the sea—I read an academic study of Cockney slang (and all of Melville's sea stories) in order to occasionally sculpt his sentences (word choice, syntax, rhythm) and those of the sailors with language appropriate for their life-world and lived, daily experience. (One of the delights of doing that was discovering just how much of the language of sailors and the sea is a part of our ordinary daily discourse, and the fresh possibilities for creating metaphors that it allows.) Now, contrast *that* language to the third-person narration in *Dreamer*, which is saturated with two millennia of theological words and concepts appropriate for the Christian vision and voice of Martin Luther King, Jr. Then contrast the voice in both of those books to that of the first-person slave narrator, Andrew Hawkins, in *Oxherding Tale*, where his language now and then is a mock version of narrators in the early English novel and, in one instance, the one we find in Laurence Sterne's *Tristram Shandy*. A *world* is invoked by each word the narrators use in those novels and, therefore, their voices are not in any way interchangeable when those narrative voices are at their purest.

We see how this works most clearly with first-person narrators, where each line of narration is also a revelation of the individual character—it is *both* narration and a character line; the narration could, in fact, be a monologue (or testimony) by a character. (See my story "Confession," a monologue in which only Tiberius speaks until the end of the story.)

However, the presence of voice—a *personality* infusing the narrative—should also be recognizable in third-person narratives where the narrator is *not* a character in the story. This can happen in two ways. First, if the story is third-person-limited to one character (usually the protagonist), the narration can occasionally employ the individuated speech of that person, i.e., when he perceives something or makes a judgment, the narrator uses his idiosyncratic diction, as happens in the story "The Education of Mingo." The second way of approaching a third-person narrator who is outside the story (like God would be if he was narrating a tale) occurs, for example, in one contemporary fiction I recall, where the narrator employs full omniscience by first physically describing a character for us, then saying, "Now let's go across town to her bank and see what's inside her safety deposit box." There, the narrator—although not a performer in the story— becomes as much of a "character" through his voice as someone in the *dramatis personae.* He can stand back from them and comment on and judge them as the narrative unfolds, and in the hands of a skillful writer this can be highly enjoyable.

Yet another approach for third-person full omniscience, one that attempts to achieve the neutral illusion of the "objective" camera's eye, is one where the writer scrubs clean all personality from the narration, but we see that in this case objectivity is an illusion because *where* one places the supposedly unbiased camera is already a decision and a judgment and a choice saturated with subjectivity.

Let me conclude this discussion on voice by saying that every fiction is experienced as a "whole." In order to discuss different aspects of a story, we only isolate them for the purpose of pedagogy. But it should be clear that any analysis of voice inevitably segues into a discussion of viewpoint, and that—like pulling a thread of a sweater—leads one to an examination of the character that particular viewpoint represents.

15. Nature Gives Us No Metaphors

*The greatest thing by far is to be a master of metaphor.
It is the one thing that cannot be learnt from others;
and it is also a sign of genius, since a good metaphor
implies an intuitive perception of the similarity in dis-
similars.*

— Aristotle, *Poetics*

*Though metaphor is seen in a highly developed form
in poetry, and is the characteristic mode of energetic
relation in poetry, it may also prove to be the radical
mode in which we correlate all our knowledge and
experience.*

—from *The Princeton Encyclopedia
of Poetry and Poetics*

During my final year in the doctoral program in philosophy
at Stony Brook, when I was churning out seminar papers and
the prospectus for my dissertation, I found it increasingly
difficult to write fiction. This wasn't a "writer's block" per
se, because I could write philosophy papers all day long. But
Western philosophers since John Locke, and especially those
acquainted with the work of Wittgenstein, harbor a deep sus-
picion of metaphor as being imprecise, sloppy, careless, and
misleading. Literary language is to be avoided. Fortunately,

during my first two quarters of teaching creative writing at the University of Washington, those reservations fell away and I was able to settle into the wisdom behind the words Albert Camus wrote in his *Notebooks* of 1935–42: "Feelings and images multiply a philosophy by ten. People can only think in images. If you want to be a philosopher, write novels."

Nature gives us no metaphors, as William Gass once said. These tropes of transference (metaphor, analogy, simile) that give us "two ideas for one" and allow us to "get hold of something fresh" (as Aristotle put it) are products of human consciousness, and as such are probably inseparable from the way the imagination and intellect operate on their highest levels, not simply in poetry but in *every* form of intellectual endeavor that I am familiar with, including the sciences. (As a heuristic, the scientists at work on subatomic particles in the 1920s advised their students to think of these strange new entities in terms of what they knew about literature and music; in the early '70s one of my editors at a newspaper called the *Southern Illinoisan* was Ben Gelman, brother of the physicist and Nobel laureate Murray Gell-Mann, a true genius who coined the term *quark*, which is a reference to a line in Joyce's *Finnegans Wake*.) I tilt somewhat toward sympathizing with anthropologists who suspect that all language is metaphor. In *Countries of the Mind* (1931), John Middleton Murry wrote, "The investigation of metaphor is curiously like the investigation of any of the primary data of consciousness. . . . Metaphor is as ultimate as speech, and speech as ultimate as thought. If we try to penetrate them beyond a certain point, we find ourselves questioning the very faculty and instrument with which we are trying to penetrate them."

Without metaphor, certain powerful, thought-provoking stories are unimaginable. For example, the extended metaphor that is Kafka's "The Metamorphosis"; or John Gardner's *Grendel* (the equating of the Beowulf monster with Sartrean existentialism); or Orwell's *Animal Farm*; or any of the animal fables from the West (Aesop) and East (Jātaka tales), among them my short story "Menagerie: A Child's Fable"; or films such as *They Shoot Horses, Don't They?* (Depression-era dance contests as a metaphor for capitalism, or at least that's how I read the story). And each and every day, our nation's inventive editorial cartoonists rely on precisely this fundamental technique as they depict the shenanigans of our elected officials. Metaphor is an essential aspect of the imagination during its peak performances across all creative and intellectual disciplines.

16. Scene and Dialogue

In one of our many exchanges, E. Ethelbert Miller asked me: "How does a fiction writer learn to write good dialogue?"

This should have been an easy question for me to stumble on. I started thinking about scenes that begin in the middle of an action or *in medias res*, which is so typical in movie and television productions. (You know, "Shoot the sheriff on the first page" to get our attention.) Then I started thinking about individual lines of dialogue—or speech between characters—as isolated phenomena, and what I liked about them. One can extract dialogue from a story and discuss in a general way its virtues. But we should remember that dialogue occurs in a context, in other words, within a specific scene. And every dramatic scene has a structure. If we have two characters, say, each enters a scene motivated by a desire or need (or conflict) that has brought him or her there. So they have (1) an *entrance*. They seldom jump right into talking about their individual motivation for being there (except in scenes that begin *in medias res*, then the writer has to explain what the heck it is we're looking at); instead they may engage in very natural and easy small talk or banter, as we find Richard Wright's characters doing at the opening of a scene in his novel *Lawd Today*:

"What you know, Skinner?"

"Don't know. What you know?"

"Don't know. How's [another character] doing?"

Or in another exchange from the same novel:
"What you saying, Jake?"
"Ain't saying."
So for a few moments (or beats) in the scene we have what is called (2) *rhythm*, the natural flow of speech between two people. At some point this will lead to (3) the *hit*, or that heightened moment in their exchange when the issue (or conflict) that has brought them together is finally revealed. (This can be a true revelation, as in the pivotal "slapping" scene in the film *Chinatown*, when the character Evelyn Mulwray reveals to the detective "Jake" Gittes that she had an incestuous relationship with her father when she was fifteen years old.) Finally, after the hit, the characters will (4) *exit* the scene. A couple of things should be noted now. First, the emotional encounter experienced by the characters in a single dramatic scene will cause them to register some degree of change psychologically, i.e., they will not exit that scene as clean as they went into it. Ideally, the scene (with its dialogue) will advance the story, moving its plot forward. So, to repeat: the structure of a dramatic scene (and usually comic ones, too) in which dialogue appears, and which determines what dialogue will be there, involves an *entrance*, *rhythm*, the *hit*, and an *exit* (from the stage or the scene).

Focusing more closely now on individual speeches, there are a few obvious points to make. Characters usually speak naturally or colloquially in short, crisp sentences. (But long speeches are, of course, sometimes required. If you want to learn how to make a character give a long speech or monologue without it being boring, do Exercise 7 in John Gardner's *The Art of Fiction* for practice; and also try your hand at Exercise 8, where you're asked to "Write a dialogue in which each of the two characters has a secret. Do not reveal the secret but make the reader intuit it. For example, the dialogue might be between a husband, who has just lost his job and hasn't worked up the courage to tell his wife, and his wife, who has a lover in the bedroom.") Ideally, those sentences should reveal character through the words the speaker uses and the specific cadence of his or her use of language. Each character's speech should be so specific to him or her that we can dispense with the label "he said." But if you must attribute a line of speech to a character, then the standard and simple "he said" will get you in less trouble than a risible choice such as "he ejaculated." (Please, don't ever write that one.) Now, take a look at this exchange from Wright's *American Hunger*:

"Can't you read really?" I asked.
"Naw," she giggled. "You know I can't read."
"You can read *some*," I said. [Italics mine.]

For me, the "some" in that sentence delivers a bit of the texture of black speech, and is more effective than, say, if the character had said "a little." Good dialogue is the product of a writer having a good ear, of listening carefully to how others speak, the words they choose, the stresses they place on certain syllables in those words. For example, in *Dreamer* I attempted to provide scansion for a line from Martin Luther King, Jr.'s sermon "A Knock at Midnight" in a scene where Chaym Smith, King's double, is trying to learn how to imitate the good doctor's individual speech patterns and where he places stress on words (see page 107).

But an even more vivid and wonderfully funny example of the music of rich ethnic speech than the three lines from Wright above can be found in the recently published novel *Ed King* by David Guterson. In this work of fiction, the protagonist is the adopted son of Daniel and Alice King, a Jewish couple, who raise him with their biological son, Simon. During one of Daniel's phone conversations (the subject is whether to let Ed know he's adopted), we have a textbook-perfect example of textured speech so convincing we almost feel we are hearing it close-range right at our ear and not reading it on the page:

> "Maybe one day they ask," said Pop. " 'How come he's tall, I'm not tall, he's got his nose, I got my nose, his hair, the other hair' — what you gonna say to your boychiks then? Huh, Dr. Dan? I'm waiting for you! This one, he's hitting home runs from the left side of the plate; the other, he's making Einstein in science class; one allergic maybe to nothing, one don't leave home without having asthma; one is this, one that, one up, one down, one yes, one no — so what do you say, Mr. Know-It-All?"
>
> "We stick with the mystery of genetics," answered Dan. "It couldn't be simpler, Pop."
>
> "Simple?" Pop said. "How is it simple? One day, he's gonna find out."
>
> "We stick with the mystery of genetics," Dan repeated. "If no one slips up or spills the beans, he isn't adopted. Let's all remember that."
>
> Pop sneezed into the phone. "Excuse me," he said. "It's lying, this business. The tooth fairy's lying, the *golem* is lying, Santa Claus lying, all of it lying, but this, Mr. Eddie, not adopted, that's *lying*, that's Number Nine of the Ten Commandments lying. Listen, Daniel, I'm telling you from my heart, you want more *tsuris* than you already got? Go ahead — tell this lie!"

Because we're talking about *dia*logue and not *mono*logue, I find my writer's notebooks of the last forty years filled with numerous examples of witty and crisp exchanges or repartee between two characters. Perhaps this is just my personal taste, but I suspect audiences for any story (in a novel or short story, in film or on stage) enjoy funny dialogue between characters, as in this back-and-forth between two characters in the philosopher George Santayana's novel *The Last Puritan*:

"Are you a Catholic?"
"No—I've lost my faith."
"Then, a Protestant?"
"Sir—I've lost my faith, not my reason."

And Charles Dickens is nothing if not a master of humorous dialogue. Here's an exchange from *Great Expectations*:

"What's the name of them things with humps?"
"Camels?"
Joe nodded. "Mrs. Camels, it was."
I supposed he meant Mrs. Camilla.

Being Buddhist, I must confess to having a great affection for those dialogue exchanges that not only make us smile but also slap us upside our heads with a spiritual lesson. Consider this famous Q&A reprinted in John C. H. Wu's *The Golden Age of Zen: Zen Masters of the T'ang Dynasty*:

"Do you perceive the fragrance of the cinnamon?"
"Yes, I do," replied Shan-ku.
Huang-lu said, "You see, I have hid nothing from you."

And from that same volume:

A monk asked, "Who is the Buddha?"
Pai-chang replied, "Who are you?"

And with that example I'll end this mini-lecture on some of the possibilities for dialogue.

17. The Importance of Plot

During my first few years of teaching the craft of writing, I came up with about twenty exercises that I would give to students returning to work with me for a second time after they had completed all thirty of the exercises in John Gardner's *The Art of Fiction*. (When I first started teaching, my students did three of these exercises a week for ten weeks, in addition to writing three stories for me and keeping a writer's notebook.) I remember several of the exercises I came up with focused on their becoming skillful with a variety of classic sentence forms (epanalepsis, anadiplosis, symploce, epistrophe, anaphora, polysyndeton, asyndeton, and the masterful long sentence). In other words, I wanted them to see the possibilities of creating elegant, architectonic structures on just the level of the sentence alone. But on the whole, and in general, I preferred in the early 1970s JG's well-conceived exercises to those of my own invention. After a decade or so, I did cut back on some of JG's exercises that were merely descriptive. (How many times can a professor actually bring himself to read student work where they attempt to "Describe a landscape as seen by a bird, but do not mention the bird"? That one gets old pretty fast.)

Over the course of three decades, a professor is likely to see changes in the elements of craft that students need to focus on. Based on those changes, I naturally emphasized some craft exercises more than others. But in my experience, the single most recurring and difficult element for apprentice writers, both graduate and undergraduate (as well as for many veterans), is plot—what literally *happens* (the external, observable, and objective action) in a story that moves it forward with a sense of organic flow. Contemporary literary stories can often be weak on that element, substituting lots of dazzle—poetic language, wit, beautiful descriptions (or "picture painting") that always bring a halt to the story's forward momentum, or at least slow it down—for tight plotting and tight pacing. For me, the simple question of *what happens next?* in a story, and the feeling of suspense this creates, is a crucial aspect of great entertainment.

Furthermore, plot, as JG wisely put it, is the storyteller's equivalent to the philosopher's argument; its importance lies in it being an interpretation (one based on causation) of *why* the world works the way it does. Occasionally, one hears literary writers dismissing the importance of plot (usually because they find good plotting hard to do), placing it in the "lesser" domain of pop (or pulp) fiction. And how many times have we heard that there are only thirty plots in the world? Or a hundred? (People give different numbers, but the point is always that plots are limited. Or that all the possible plots have already been written.) I've never believed any of those excuses for justifying stories that are weak on plot. (There *are*, of course, stories with minimal plots that are wonderful, but I think you see the point I'm making.)

So during my last twenty years of teaching, I required that students turn in one new, fully developed plot outline (two single-spaced pages) every week. (Back in the late '70s, I briefly made myself do this exercise, too.) In part, this was to discourage them from relying on the same story line over and over again. It was to encourage them to become raconteurs, writers able to effortlessly create a new story on demand. And also so that, even though they wrote only three stories for me during every ten-week quarter, they left class with seven more developed plot outlines they could use for stories after my class ended, on their own or in another workshop.

In my classes, we always began with a student critiquing the work before us for that particular day. But before that student launched into his (or her) discussion of a story written by another, I required that he (or she) first break down or present the story in terms of just its plot. And to do that with just *five to seven* sentences. (I didn't want to hear about theme or ideas, character traits, or any of that, only about *what happens*, then *what happens next*.) You have no idea how difficult some students found this to do, though the literal plot of *any* story can be summarized in fewer than ten sentences. (I can usually do this in four or five sentences, though I need something like eight for the plot of Ellison's episodic *Invisible Man*.) And, as I believe Aristotle suggested in the *Poetics*, just the bare-bones summary of a terrific story should move a listener to experience pity and fear. Try doing this yourself with one of your favorite novels, short stories, television episodes, or films. It should quickly give you the basic, minimal, underlying structure—the skeleton, the spine—upon which everything else (all the literary richness and elaboration) in the story rests.

18. Storytelling and
the Alpha Narrative

Potter at the wheel.
From centering to finished pot.
Form increases as options decrease.
Softness goes to hardness.
　　　　　—Deng Ming-Dao

By now I'm sure I've read thousands of novels and short stories, by students and professionals both. I've been a fiction judge three times for the National Book Awards (twice chairing that panel), three times for the Pulitzer Prize, once for the PEN/Faulkner, twice for the Los Angeles Times Book Prize, and I've judged so many other contests that I can no longer remember them all. The funny thing about being a teacher—especially a teacher of writing—is that you develop the habit of reading from start to finish what*ever* anyone puts in front of you, whether you like it or not, with your red pencil in hand, because your job is to grade and comment on it. But when those contest books arrive on my doorstep via UPS, and I open the boxes and spread out in front of me on the living room floor approximately three hundred novels and story collections, I'm confronted with the same question over and over again—a question that reaches all the way back to my teens. With all these books before me, where do I *start*? What do I really *want* to read? And each time I face this dilemma, I come to the same realization. I *don't* necessarily want to start with *this* bestselling book by a famous author. Or *that* book, which had a huge publicity campaign behind it. Nor am I interested in a book because it has an award attached to it. Or because a teacher told me I should read it. Or because it's about timely social or political issues. And I'm certainly not interested because someone says that *every*body is reading it, and therefore I should read it, too, so I can discuss that book when it comes up in a conversation.

No, when I stare at that pile of three hundred books sent by the Pulitzer committee or the National Book Foundation, what I do is try for a moment to *forget* absolutely everything I've learned about literature in the last fifty years. I want to forget all the critical and aesthetic theories. I want to forget all that I know as a teacher of writing and all I've experienced as a writer publishing since I was seventeen. What I'm saying is that when I begin looking through those books, what I'm *hungering* for is the same innocent enchantment I had when I was a reader of twelve or thirteen. At that age, when I turned to the first page of a novel or a story, I knew *nothing* at all about the writer, his (or her) previous works, or whether the book was literary or pulp fiction. I didn't know what was good writing or bad. All I knew, at age thirteen, was that sometimes when I stumbled upon a story, my experience from the first page—in fact, from the first sentence—was that a kind of spell was cast over me. It was the experience of mystery and wonder and needing to know *what happens next*, often after hearing that powerful opening phrase *Once upon a time*. In the midst of this enchantment, I didn't want to stop reading or go to bed or do *any*thing else until I'd learned how events in the story unfolded, because I was *certain* the outcome had meaning for my own life.

Forty years later this is still the experience I want when I turn to a novel or a story. In works such as these, one *never* has the feeling that a writer is *trying* to tell a story. We aren't even aware of the writer, only of the compelling world he (or she) has delivered to us. For twenty years now I've been trying to get a handle on how to describe the magic of this experience. I don't even have a name for the kind of story I'm talking about, but I will try to give it one.

Two years ago I thought I'd see what my graduate students had to say about this matter. I went to class and before we settled down to work, I said, "Can anyone tell me the difference between a *writer* and a *storyteller*?" My younger students seemed baffled by that question. However, there was a man in that class who was a retired English professor, and an author who published one of the first Vietnam novels in the late '60s. (He was auditing my class.) When none of the other class members spoke up, he raised his hand and simply said, "I'd much rather have dinner with a storyteller than a writer."

I think this distinguished gentleman—his name is George Sidney and his 1969 novel is called *For the Love of Dying*— gave us something to think about. All the technique, craft, and literary theory we accumulate as writers *must* be in the service of that most deceptively simple and yet most difficult of achievements—delivering undamaged a whopping good, imaginative, and original story. A story *so* good that what Aristotle says about plays in his *Poetics* also applies to this fiction: "The plot should be so constructed that even without seeing the play, anyone hearing of the incidents happening thrills with fear and pity as a result of what occurs." A story of which we can say what John Gardner said of Pär Lagerkvist's novel *The Holy Land*, that it compressed the complexity and difficulty of modern life "into a few stark and massive symbols in which all our experience and all human history are locked." For want of a better phrase, I would call a story of this kind an Alpha Narrative. And as a writer, I find that these kinds of stories humble me. They are stories that endure, hold us in suspense, and liberate our perception.

I first experienced this kind of story when I was a teenager and read Shakespeare's *Romeo and Juliet*, a story that can be traced back to the Greek romance of *Anthia and Habrocomes* in the second century. It was apparently first told in modern Europe in 1470 by Masuccio in his *Novellino*, and was later adapted by Luigi da Porto in his novel *La Giulietta* in 1535, and by Bandello in his *Novelle* in 1554. So there are many versions, many interpretations—with numerous ones after Shakespeare's—yet at the center of this Alpha Narrative there is the most simple of story lines, one that is elegant, not sloppy or inefficient.

So my question is, how, as writers, do we discover such a narrative? To put this another way, many of the students I've worked with in twenty-eight years want to be writers *before* they have a compelling story to tell. To give you an example of just how rare such stories are, consider for a moment those writers who are blessed to live a long life, have very productive careers, and produce many, many good books.

In the early twentieth century, Aldous Huxley and D. H. Lawrence had two of the largest bodies of work among English writers. Of all their books, which ones do you remember? I would wager that for Huxley the title that comes to mind is *Brave New World*, and for Lawrence perhaps *Sons and Lovers* or *Lady Chatterley's Lover*. Or think about George Orwell, who wrote many books about English life. What most people will think of when Orwell's name is mentioned are *1984* and *Animal Farm*.

One of my friends with whom I speak often about fiction, classical or contemporary, is Michael Anderson, for eighteen years one of the editors at the *New York Times Book Review*. He tells me that as an editor he had to go through twelve to fifteen books a week before assigning them to reviewers. Michael, a very smart man, feels (and I feel, too) that often a writer like the ones I just mentioned must sometimes work a lifetime before he (or she) stumbles upon that *one* story that becomes an archetype for our thoughts, feelings, and experiences—you can often see a writer's early books prefiguring or partially realizing that one story he is searching for, as is the case with Melville's early work leading up to *Moby-Dick*. If a writer during a long career hits that kind of story *once*—says Michael Anderson— then that writer *has* been treated well by the gods. If he or she delivers this kind of baby *twice*, we are looking at a true major talent. And if the writer creates such a story *three* times or better (like Shakespeare or Mark Twain), then such an author *has* to be considered one of the towering literary giants of his (and perhaps all) time. Some writers, of course, are blessed with such a pure story performance only once—I'm thinking of Ralph Ellison's *Invisible Man*—but as I said, "only once" can be enough if one's goal is to enrich literary culture.

Now, the question you are probably asking is the same one I ask myself every day when I sit down to write: What *makes* such a story? What do they have in common?

Every Alpha Narrative I know about offers a strong example of what John Barth calls the "ground situation," a fictional premise where something interesting and important is at stake, a premise so rich it will take the writer a whole book to fully unpack and explore all its multileveled dimensions.

I hate to use one of my own novels, *Middle Passage*, as an example, but as poor an example as it may be, it might still shed some light on why a fictional premise should be rich in imaginative possibilities. The "ground situation" in *Middle Passage* is the voyage of a slave ship. The first questions I had to ask myself were: Who are the people on this ship? What personal motivations brought each member of the crew— from the captain to the cabin boy—onboard for a voyage intended to transfer African slaves to America? Furthermore, who *are* these Africans, individually? In all the stories I'd read about the slave trade, such as Melville's "Benito Cereno," the Africans were never presented individually as people with complexity—they were simply a mass of suffering humanity, like cattle, unnamed and unvoiced. I wondered: Who were they before they were captured? What were their lives like in their village? What social roles did each have before Europeans came? What was their religion, their language, their customs, their *dreams*? And the same questions had to be asked, of course, about the ship's captain, who turned out to be a diminutive version of Sir Richard Francis Burton combined with Jack London's Wolf Larsen in *The Sea Wolf*: a man who was a genius, an imperialist, a racist yet was fascinating to me because his personality was prismatic. In other words, in this novel, Captain Ebenezer Falcon opens the "ground situation" onto the entire history of the sea adventure story stretching back to *The Voyage of Argo* by Apollonius of Rhodes and to the Sinbad stories, to name just a couple. The presence of the Africans, the Allmuseri, in the "ground situation" provides a doorway for exploring non-Western philosophies and spiritual traditions not based on the metaphysical dualism represented by Captain Falcon. And the narrator and protagonist, Rutherford Calhoun, is the story's bridge to all the possibilities of a picaresque antihero, a free black man, somewhat irresponsible at the start of the story, whose character carries echoes of Ishmael and Odysseus.

So there is the "ground situation." There are the *dramatis personae*. There is the simple story line, a voyage. Put them all together on the sea (which in this novel symbolizes the Void in Buddhism), put them in a dilapidated ship that represents the racial diversity of contemporary America, throw in the possibility of storms, slave revolts, a mutiny by the crew, an African god that sits in the hold of the ship like a nuclear bomb ready to go off, add Rutherford Calhoun's "Cain and Abel" conflict with his brother Jackson, add his love for a schoolteacher named Isadora Bailey, and also his longing to find a place that he can truly call "home," and we have—front-loaded in this fiction—a "ground situation," or fictional premise where *any*thing can happen; where it is man versus Nature, man versus man, and man versus himself; where the writer stays in a state of suspense and must keep probing and asking the right questions; and where what is at stake—for Rutherford and I hope the reader— is the perennial, open-ended question "How in heaven's name shall we live in a world smothered by suffering?"

Aristotle's term for this creative process of unpacking a story premise is *energeia*, "the actualization of the potential that exists in character and situation." I think the methodical actualization of the potential in an Alpha Narrative happens this way:

Every story begins with some sort of problem or "conflict." If for some reason you don't like that word, we can say that when the story opens our protagonist finds himself (or herself) in a state of disequilibrium. It is possible to begin a story with the character in a state of equilibrium, but he or she must soon find that state of affairs disturbed: there is something the protagonist wants, needs, or desires. There is something missing in his world, and he must acquire it; or something has intruded upon his world, and he must deal with *that* in order to regain equilibrium. And this cannot be any old conflict the writer wishes to attach to his character. As a conflict, it must be anchored in the specificity and texture of the character's background and biography. Something else important to say is that we have chosen *this* particular moment in a character's life to dramatize because it is at *this* moment that the character is living for high stakes. The key word here is *change*. The "ground situation" propels the protagonist into a *process of transformation*. He—and the reader—cannot come out of the Alpha Narrative as clean as when they went in. This is the very definition of what we mean when we say that a character is "round," not "flat." He is "round" because during the story, and based on its events, he is forced to *evolve*. (And so must all the other major characters in the story.) In this sense, we can say that in the Alpha Narrative, plot and character are perfectly united, because character is the *engine* of plot. The conflict, or "ground situation," arises from the specificity of this particular individual, and it is the first *good idea* the writer has, the one that sets everything else in motion.

I always tell my students that in this first stage of the story the reader and writer find themselves in the realm of *possibility*. The writer has countless choices he can make as he decides who his characters are, what conflicts they have, and what sort of world they inhabit. But with *each* sentence, with *each* detail he places on the page, he *despoils* those possibilities. This gradual limiting of the possible occurs as the writer wonders, "Given *this* character in *this* situation and with *this* specific problem to solve, what might happen next?"

Well, what happens is the protagonist attempts to resolve his (or her) problem—if he succeeds, that's the end of the story. (And maybe also the end of your career.) So the writer's job is to constantly frustrate him. Perhaps his attempt to overcome whatever conflict he has opens into a larger and more difficult problem, or he comes to realize that his initial problem was far more complex than he ever dreamed. By this time we are no longer in the realm of possibility. We are now in the middle of the story—in the realm of *probability*—where all the details and decisions the writer made in the beginning create a causal connection and profluence between events, a connection that we, as readers, feel is logical and inevitable based on all that has come before. Here, in the middle of the tale, it is crucial that a writer comes up with a *second good idea*, one that deepens and further complicates the actualization of the

111

potential contained in the story's premise. For a reader (and often for the writer) this second good idea is *never* experienced as predictable—we never feel, there in the middle of the story, that we saw this new series of developments coming. Yet despite our surprise over "what happens next," the reader feels this new dramatic territory in the story flows organically from all the events that preceded it. Most likely, the writer himself didn't fully see the events in the middle of the story until he *got* there. In other words, if the writer is faithful to the minute details he has established in the beginning, if he is tracing carefully every nuance of character and situation—How does Captain Falcon eat? What eccentricities does the first mate, Peter Cringle, have? What superstitious rituals do sailors follow when they're at sea?—then he will be continually surprised by how the actors in his story are behaving. If he is *not* surprised by their behavior, by what they say and do in the middle of the story, then I doubt that his readers will be surprised either. If he's not surprised, he's not asking enough hard questions. The excitement and suspense of discovery must be there for the writer *first*—you get up every day burning to get back to your computer just so you can see what this ensemble of characters is going to do next, and to one another.

Ideally, as the writer moves toward the end of an Alpha Narrative, he feels as if he isn't creating or making up anything at all. At this point, the story has entered the realm of pure *necessity*, where events play themselves out with all the rigor of a logical proof. Here, at the end, the writer is more like a witness or a reporter than someone who is "trying" to tell a story—all he's doing now is transcribing what he sees unfolding before his mind's eye. The only things that can happen are things predestined by the decisions the writer made in chapter one. This final phase of the story also requires a third and last *good idea* to wrap things up, but by this time—after all that has transpired—the writer should be able to find that idea with ease.

The structure that I've just outlined resembles a funnel, large and wide at the beginning when we are in the realm of possibility, and quite small at the end when the potential of the story's premise has been exhausted. This is a structure that all storytellers know by instinct. Books on how to write fiction always try to explain this creative process, but usually they fail. The process is all about asking questions, digging deeper into character and event. In my experience, I find that when a novel fails, or when students get stuck in their stories and can't figure out *what happens next*, it's almost always because they failed to fully define—and understand—the character and his conflict and the "ground situation" in the beginning; or the story might fail because in the middle the writer hasn't conjured a second *good idea* inherent in his material; or, finally, the story may fail at the end because the writer by now is just exhausted and imposes on his characters events that have not grown logically and systematically and organically from all that came before.

As writers, we live for the moment when the Powers That Be hand us a story so rich that exploring it fully becomes the most legal fun we can have. I see the techniques and elements of craft I've taught writing students at UW as simply tools to prepare them for the time when such a narrative drops onto their laps. But for that to happen, they must see themselves, first and foremost, as storytellers. I want the finding of Alpha Narratives, and the process of fictional discovery, to become second nature for them. Because I know that if they accomplish this, if this way of *conceiving* a story becomes a habit, then a way of life, technique, will take care of itself, and they will create stories that will be read and talked about and even retold when their own great-great-grandchildren are very, very old.

19. On the Novel
and Short Story

There's many a bestseller that could have been pre-
vented by a good teacher.
— Flannery O'Connor

The garden-variety novel is quite easy to create, and that, of course, is the reason so many people can write them, especially formula fictions such as murder mysteries, second-rate horror and science fiction, and romance novels. I once had a student who made a decent living writing romance novels, and she explained the very strict rules of plotting and characterization required by her publisher; readers of those kinds of novels, she informed me, whip through three a day (one after breakfast, another in the afternoon, and a third before going to bed) since the boilerplate for the stories varies little from book to book. John Gardner once wrote that in order to write good junk fiction, one has to have a good junk mind. My friend the writer Fred Pfeil (author of *Goodman 2020*) once referred to novels of this kind as "industrial fiction." As I've noted before, this kind of writing pays a publisher's electric bills and helps writers put their kids through school, so it does have some value.

In my case, I wrote six novels in two years before *Faith and the Good Thing* (1970 through 1972), one every ten weeks, ten pages a day, five days a week. The basic tools for writing a novel are really just a few—characters, plot, (dramatic) scenes, description, and narration. These tools can be learned by anyone in a short period of time. One of the great virtues of the novel, as a literary form, is that a writer has room to create an entire, very detailed fictional universe and people it with as many characters as he or she pleases. Another virtue is that the novel is capacious enough to contain other, shorter literary forms within itself. Indeed, it can contain whatever you want. As Ishmael Reed once said, "a novel can be the six o'clock news."

So the garden-variety novel is not much of an intellectual or artistic challenge. Again, this is why we have so many of them. (Clarence Major once said one meaning of "novel" in French is a "new thing," and, yes, I believe each novel should be that—something we have not exactly seen before.) But even the "literary" novel runs the risk of what the French call *remplissage*, or "literary padding," to fill up pages. There's almost nothing more boring that I can think of than seeing a novelist pad out an underimagined work that has a slim premise, no more complexity than a child's primer, Styrofoam people who are sociological problems masquerading as characters, not much of a story, is thin in imagery and thought, and contains no artistic or intellectual surprises. Oh, wait, there is something more boring: spending three hundred or four hundred pages with characters you don't enjoy hanging out with and for whom you couldn't care less about "what happens next" to them.

By contrast, a well-wrought short story demands—like a poem—a rigor, discipline, compression, and economy not always found in the garden-variety novel, where padding, the lack of careful plotting, verbosity, thin or stereotypical characters, and poor pacing can be absorbed and made (barely) acceptable simply by the novel's length. (Or the length can cause us to not see that lack of rigor.) The flaws of excess and slippages in focus that we forgive in the novel are simply not permitted in the finely crafted short story, a form capable of creating in its unique format, where every paragraph and sentence is as essential as elements in an equation, the perception-altering insights and lasting emotional impression that most novels strive for but usually fail to achieve. There, in the short story, our emphasis is on originality, ingenuity, economy, and unity of form in a construction that is logical, efficient, and harmonious in its parts. Usually, it offers us a single predominant character, and a single predominant event. And, as Edgar Allan Poe (who just about single-handedly invented the modern short story) pointed out in essays such as "On the Aim and Technique of the Short Story" (1842), it can be experienced in a single sitting.

So, in my view, both novels and short stories, as forms, have their strengths and weaknesses. Clearly, for either to be effective they must have a compelling, original *story* as their foundation. There's no reason to write in either literary form unless one has a special story worthy of an intelligent, learned, and sophisticated reader's time and attention.

20. The Essay

E. Ethelbert Miller says: Let's talk about the essay form. What makes for a good essay? Where have the ideas for your essays come from? Do people (magazines/newspapers) request them? Have you been moved to write an essay because of something you've read or an event in your life? Who do you admire or respect when it comes to the essay writer? What is a good length for an essay? What role might philosophy play in shaping the content of an essay?

Let me start my answer for this question by repeating something a reviewer said of my essays in *Turning the Wheel: Essays on Buddhism and Writing*. He said I was a superior essayist, but not a great one. I think that judgment is fair. The essay as a literary form comes easily to me. About 50 percent of my body of published work is nonfiction (or the essay.)

But I'm not a great essayist, nor have I worked at being one. A truly *great* American essayist is someone like James Baldwin, who gave us perhaps a dozen essays that will forever define a certain dimension of the American experience. (Like many critics, I feel his essays are superior to his fiction, though his first novel, *Go Tell It on the Mountain*, is worth discussing for historical reasons.) Baldwin's essays, in addition to being beautiful performances of language, pack a rare emotional power. I work to get emotion into my fiction, but in my essays and articles I'm not emotional, just professorial in my effort to clarify a subject, first for myself, then hopefully for a reader. At best, my work in the essay form might be called meditational.

This work came about probably as an extension of my background in journalism when (briefly) I was a newspaper reporter, columnist, and features writer in Illinois in the late 1960s and early '70s. Philosophy is also a contributing factor to the essays I've written insofar as in the early 1980s I made a strong effort to teach myself how to write philosophically for popular magazines; in other words, finding ways to express often esoteric concepts without using the tribal languages employed in philosophy seminars and academic publications for specialists. I believe the first work where I managed to successfully do that was "Philosophy and Black Fiction," published in *Obsidian* in 1980. And, of course, in the essays I've written for popular Buddhist magazines what I attempt to do is present philosophical concepts and experiences with accuracy and clarity in a way that is also reader-friendly. What Edgar Allan Poe said of the short story probably applies to the essay: namely, it likely works most effectively as an experience if it can be read in a single sitting. And for me, what I value in the essays I read (and hope occurs in the ones I write) is the fact that the writer has offered me the opportunity to carefully and methodically think or reason along with him or her about a particular subject.

One of the most famous quotes we have from Karl Marx is "The philosophers have only interpreted the world, in various ways; the point, however, is to change it."

When I first read that as a young philosophy student, I enjoyed its activist thrust, but somewhere in the back of my mind I kept thinking, "Just how *well* have we interpreted this world?" That, in essence, is what I try to do daily as an artist—the effort to interpret and better understand the world around me, to bring it some clarity. Sometimes the interpretation is best rendered as a short story. Sometimes as a novel or drawing. Or in essay or screenplay form. I've never privileged or prioritized one form of expression over another. And, as a footnote to Marx, I think we can say that artistic (and philosophical) interpretations have, down through history, changed lives through the liberation of perception.

21. The Risks We Take

In my writing workshops, whenever it was necessary to discuss the issue of characterization, I would explain to my students what they needed to know about their main or central characters. Some of my advice was standard fare. For example, that one's protagonist (*and* the story's reader) should not come out of the story as clean as when he or she went in. The conflict and its development will force the protagonist to undergo change, to evolve. I told my students they must know as much about their character as Lajos Egri indicates in the biographical questions he says writers must ask, in the "Bone Structure" section that appears in his classic work *The Art of Dramatic Writing* (1942). As an exercise, I'd ask them to write their main character's obituary. And then I'd ask them to do something that always caused a few students in the room to visibly squirm.

I asked them to determine what their protagonist most feared in this world. I told them I didn't mean snakes or spiders. No, I meant his or her deepest *social* fear. The one situation they most dreaded experiencing. The one event they would prefer to die than have to face. Then I told them they should maneuver their protagonist into exactly that situation to see what happens—if, in fact, he or she is destroyed by it, or is changed by it and in what ways. Everyone in class knew what doing that would require. They knew what I was asking of them. They saw that in literary art, you have to pay a price and take personal inventory. They would have to delve deeply into the most tender, raw, and painful places in themselves and identify their *own* deepest social fears.

In some of my novels and stories I've had to do that when the story demanded it. That is, to give to one of my characters an excruciatingly painful experience from my past or the life of someone close to me. There is such a passage in "The Sorcerer's Apprentice," and when I wrote it tears were falling from my eyes onto the typewriter keys. (Earlier in my life, there was nothing more dreadful to me, a good Confucian son, than the thought of failing my father and mother, letting them down after all the sacrifices they had made for me, and in this story that is exactly what the protagonist must suffer through.)

There is another in *Dreamer*—a passage where one of the main characters (Matthew Bishop) remembers when he and his mother traveled south during the era of segregation and were hungry, and the humiliation she received (that any black person would have received) at a white roadside diner, but even that, Matthew sees, cannot diminish his mother's dignity and innate nobility. To a somewhat lesser degree, writing about the details of my mother's death, and the feeling I had of being orphaned, was a small step in the exercise of deliberately baring my soul on the page.

These are emotionally important moments in fiction. I believe they transcend what normally passes for analysis in literary criticism (for example, structuralism, semiotics, deconstruction) because they are so raw, and in no way cerebral or intellectualized. Their power is primal. Pure, unadulterated feeling beyond concepts. Beyond theory. No teacher or mentor can help a student achieve this. These are intentional risks of the heart, not craft. They are a giving on the page of what is not easy to give. It seems to me that most of these moments take place in our childhoods, when we were most vulnerable. Describing those episodes, a writer must open himself or herself, become emotionally naked, brutally honest, and trace with infinite care every laceration, wound, and scar to the best of his (or her) ability in order to get it right, to finally externalize it on the page and liberate himself from it. And all of that is, of course, in the service of the story. In the greater service of literature.

This kind of writing takes a certain kind of courage. (And also, I think, takes a toll on the writer, takes a chunk out of him or her emotionally.) I am not as good at this as many writers I admire. Foremost among these is James Alan McPherson, for whom brutal emotional honesty is a hallmark. In one memorable story he describes the denial of his father's genius during the era of segregation (he came up with an invention that whites would not allow him to give to the world), the devastating toll that took on him (alcoholism, being thrown in jail overnight), and a scene toward that essay's end when father and son are literally united by electricity—his father is repairing a light fixture, sticks one hand into the socket, has his son's hand in the other, and the son is holding an object to ground them both. If either of them lets go, the other (or both of them) will die. And in that transcendent scene, as electricity and the elemental power of the universe courses through them, the black father looks down at his son and quietly says, "I would never hurt you."

McPherson has achieved this kind of leave-you-shattered-in-your-seat magic time and again in his short stories and essays. Little wonder then that on October 12, 2012, he—a recipient of the Pulitzer Prize for one of his short-story collections, and one of the first MacArthur Fellows—was honored with a tribute at the Englert Theatre in Iowa City at which he received the first Paul Engle Prize, which "honors an individual who, like Paul Engle (a longtime director of the Iowa Writers' Workshop), represents a pioneering spirit in the world of literature through writing, editing, publishing, or teaching, and whose active participation in the larger issues of the day has contributed to the betterment of the world through the literary arts."

Emotional honesty such as we find in McPherson's well-crafted work is an achievement more than deserving of such honors and awards.

What Helps the Writer?

22. On Teachers and Mentors

There is a great difference between teachers and mentors. When I was fifteen years old, I studied with the cartoonist/ writer Lawrence Lariar in his two-year correspondence course, which today we would probably call distance learning. He was prolific (something I admired), the author of more than a hundred books, some of these being murder mysteries he wrote under a couple of pseudonyms. He was cartoon editor of *Parade* magazine, of the Best Cartoons of the Year series, and at one time he was an "idea man" (not an animator) at Disney studios. I "found" Lariar when I was fourteen years old and had the only serious argument I ever had with my father when I announced to him that I planned on a career as an artist.

Later, during my senior year in high school, I was accepted at an art school in Illinois, then bailed out at the last minute— in May 1966—when I decided I couldn't gamble the hard-earned money my dad was paying for my college education on a career that might be financially questionable. I was, after all, the first member of my family to go to college. So I went downstate to the only school still admitting students in late spring and majored in journalism, which gave me the chance to draw—and, as it turned out, write. Decades later, I relished the years my daughter went to Cornish College of the Arts in Seattle, because she was living my teenage dream, and I could drool over her textbooks.

But when I told my father my plans at age fourteen, he said, "Chuck, they don't let black people do that." His words were simply unacceptable to me. If I couldn't draw, I didn't want to live. Back then, I read *Writer's Digest* for its profiles on famous cartoonists, and I came across an ad for Lariar's course. I wrote him a letter, explaining what my dad had said, and asked him if he agreed with that. Lariar fired back a letter to me within a week. (He was a liberal Jewish man living on Long Island, who changed his last name in the 1930s, I guess, and once delighted in infuriating his neighbors by having black artists over to his house for drawing lessons.) In his letter, he said, "Your father is *wrong*. You can do whatever you want with your life. All you need is a good teacher."

My father backed down, admitting that when it came to the arts in the 1960s, he didn't know what the hell he was talking about, and he paid for my lessons with Lariar between 1963 and 1965. During those two years when I was still in high school, I'd take the Greyhound bus from Illinois to New York, stay with my relatives in Brooklyn for a week, and, wearing a suit and tie, pound the pavement in Manhattan with my "swatch" (samples) from one publishing house to another, looking for work. (It was during one of those meetings that I met a young editor/cartoonist, Charles Barsotti, who was very encouraging to me when I was a kid, and published regularly in *The New Yorker*, which tragically has a history of not using the work of black cartoonists.)

Friends of mine have often told me that they wanted to be writers since they were five years old. That was never me. I knew from an early age that I was good at writing, sure, and writing was fun. On weekends when I was an undergraduate, I use to write the term papers for other students in my dorm when they wanted to party, five dollars per paper. Money back guaranteed if they failed to get an A. I never had to return those payments, and the assignments I did for them meant later I would become a writer and they wouldn't. However, from kidhood forward all that I was *burning* to do was draw. Visual artists (then later philosophers) have always been my heroes. Those were the first two tribes I belonged to. I can say that of only about a handful of writers. There are, of course, many, many writers I greatly respect, but my passions for art and philosophy predate my entry into the world of "creative writing."

During those New York trips, I naturally visited Lariar, who fixed me lunch (when I was in my teens) or dinner (when my wife, newborn son, and I visited him during my time at Stony Brook University). He loaded me up with original art from the days when he had a syndicated strip (he wrote, someone else drew it), and regaled me with stories about the comic artists I so admired. In college, I sent him copies of every editorial, panel cartoon, comic strip, and illustration I published (between 1965 and 1972 there were more than a thousand of these publications in Illinois periodicals, the *Chicago Tribune*, black magazines such as *Jet*, *Ebony*, *Black World*, *Players*, and some risqué places I dare not mention and would like to forget), and he'd always write back something encouraging.

My 1970 PBS series, *Charlie's Pad*, was based on his two-year course, and inspired by a TV spot he did in the 1950s when at the end of a news program he drew something funny about that day's headlines. When he read *Faith and the Good Thing*, he wrote me a letter, saying, "You have the 'touch.'" I still have a box of old correspondence with Lariar, who died in 1981, the same year as my mother and the year my daughter was born. I recently described this relationship with Lariar in greater detail in the essay "My Father's Pillow Talk," published in *Epoch* in the fall of 2014.

But while Lariar was a fine teacher, John Gardner was a true *mentor*. When I decided to take an introductory class

Gardner offered in the fall of 1972, "Professional Writing" (which I went to only once, preferring to meet with him in his office to discuss my work, since I'd already written six novels before *Faith and the Good Thing*), I read *Grendel*, which at the time was newly published. I would never take something as important as an art course without first seeing if the (literary) artist was someone I might be able to get along with. I was at that time finishing a master's degree in philosophy and supporting myself by working part-time on the *Southern Illinoisan*, writing news stories, features, obits, a weekly column, farm news, drawing editorial cartoons and illustrations, and proofreading the Sunday paper for eight hours on Saturday night, all for the princely sum of $50 a week, which I supplemented by drawing twenty-five panel cartoons each week as a freelancer, and usually selling about five, which paid for our weekly groceries when I was in grad school. (My wife, then an elementary school teacher, was obviously doing the bulk of supporting both of us.) I was impressed by Gardner's credentials as a medievalist, by his interest in thinkers such as R. G. Collingwood and Alfred North Whitehead (and, of course, his constant disagreements with Sartre), his devotion to writing, and his appreciation for the religion of my childhood, Christianity. (Gardner's father in upstate New York had been something of a preacher, and Gardner drifted into medieval studies because of his love of Chaucer and the religion that animated that artist's vision.) To be perfectly honest here, I'm sure I could never have apprenticed myself in a highly personal, one-on-one relationship to a writer who was irreligious or indifferent (or hostile) to all the historical richness offered by humanity's spiritual traditions.

We hit it off when I was writing *Faith*—he thought my characters had "dignity" and liked the storyteller voice in that novel, and my being in philosophy. Early in our relationship, I saw how other students were constantly asking for his support, so I made a point of never asking him for anything. But he took me under his wing anyway, generously helping me at every turn. Again, to be honest here, I have to say that since I was in philosophy and training for a career in that field, the literary book world was of very little (or no) interest to me. I just wanted to write the books I felt needed to be written. A "career" in creative writing was not only the farthest thing from my mind, but I was actually turned off by the negative "wild and crazy" things I'd read over the years about the "writer's life."

Even today I have slightly the same attitude, I suppose. The joy of creating—writing, drawing—is everything for me, but the "careerist" aspects of the profession have always left me cold. They don't mean much to me. Unlike some writers I know, I'm not looking for love (or even approval) through my work—I got loads of that from my parents, and after that from my wife and children. So I can't be bought, and I can't be bullied. Once a work is done I do my best to avoid the literary spotlight, to quietly return to the demands of family life and the daily creative regimen I've maintained for decades. And I'm liable sometimes to create something for free, or for an obscure publication, simply because I'm excited about and believe in the project or feel that creative contribution is for a good cause. (Thank God for my literary agents, who protect me from that tendency in myself.)

Nevertheless, Gardner after *Grendel* (which won him critical praise) and 1972's *Sunlight Dialogues* (his first bestseller) brought me into the book world. He was becoming famous, and he was generous toward his students, perhaps because for fifteen years he experienced so much rejection of his own work. Once or twice he canceled our conferences because he was traveling back and forth to teach at Northwestern University. Returning from one of these trips, he smiled from ear to ear and thrust into my hands an issue of a Chicago-based publication called *Fiction Midwest*. The lead piece was my first chapter of *Faith*, which Gardner had submitted without telling me. "Now," he said, "you're published." He talked to everyone about the novel before I finished it, assuring me, "Don't worry, I won't let you make a mistake."

I took notes on even his casual remarks about fiction, and ordered all his earlier works of criticism. Not only did he engineer my first "serious" literary publication, but Gardner orchestrated my first public reading as well. In the spring of 1973, he convinced me to appear with him and eight other writers he knew and nurtured. The thought of reading before an audience terrified me. I asked, "What should I do?" Gardner shrugged and simply replied, "Eh, you put on a mask."

When *Faith* was finished, Gardner referred me to his agency, the best in America, Georges Borchardt, Inc., which has represented all my work since 1973. When I was at Stony Brook University, working on my PhD in philosophy, we were chatting by phone in 1974 and he casually mentioned he'd be reading at Hofstra. Then he said, "*Be* there." So we were, my wife, Joan, and I, sitting down front beside his first wife (also named Joan) in the audience as he read from his fiction. Then he said he had something better to read, and—to my shock—brought out his copy of *Faith*. I squirmed down in my seat.

Gardner put my name forward for a dozen teaching posts even before I could take my PhD qualifying exams, and the letter of reference he wrote for me in 1976 when I applied for an appointment at the University of Washington (which I never saw) is, my colleagues told me, a classic example of a literary lion using all his celebrity and clout to clear a way for his former student.

In 1977, Len Randolph at the NEA was talking to two filmmakers from WGBH/Boston, Fred Barzyk and Olivia Tappan, who were looking for a black writer to script a screenplay about the oldest living American, Charlie Smith, then 137. Gardner told Randolph they should call me; that reference led to twenty years of teleplay- and screenwriting for PBS and, later, Hollywood studios. One of my most anthologized short stories, "Exchange Value," is a piece Gardner published in the 1981 issue of *Choice* that he edited, then he included it in *Best American Short Stories* as a guest editor. Another much reprinted story, "China," he published in his literary journal, *MSS*, after we'd been arguing back and forth about my increasing movement toward Buddhism, a religion he—very Protestant, very Western—once told me he felt was "wrong," though later he softened his stance in an introduction called "Meditational Fiction" he wrote for *Tengu Child*, a collection of stories by Kikuo Itaya that he edited and translated with Nobuko Tsukui. ("Since we are not Buddhists, one might ask, why should we read the stories of Itaya, a writer not widely read even in his native Japan?" he wrote. "The easy and immediate answer is because they're beautiful.")

But even the best of literary apprenticeships, those based on love and mutual respect, can have drawbacks. The elder artist, if his personality and gifts are as strong as Gardner's were, may have problems with new directions his student may take. Through his example of generosity, he showed me how to work with my own students for thirty-three years, always putting their interests and needs first, helping them get published, and so forth. There was no falling out between us—that could never be. Indeed, toward the end Gardner was still urging me to come to SUNY Binghamton and teach there with him, even saying if his department couldn't find the funds for an academic line, he'd put up his own salary to bring me there. But with *Oxherding Tale* I desperately needed to push beyond his conception at the time of what black literature and culture (and Charles Johnson) should be. When he read that manuscript and responded to it—we were

meeting at his home in Susquehanna County, Pennsylvania—
he said with a bit of uncharacteristic bafflement, "This is a
different Charles Johnson."

Not different, really. As a young writer, I composed *Faith*
with the intention of getting a rise out of Gardner and showing him what I could do, all that I'd managed to master on
my own. With *Oxherding Tale*, on the other hand, I was writing the "platform" novel, as I call it, that I would build the
rest of my writing life on, the novel with which our intellectual and artistic paths would diverge. Although we never
saw eye-to-eye on Buddhism, he called my publisher for that
novel just before its release and asked if he could endorse the
book—"words," as the critic Roger Sale pointed out, that
were "among the last John Gardner wrote" before his fatal
motorcycle accident on September 14, 1982.

If one must choose a mentor, I think it's important to identify precisely what that elder artist can offer in the way of
objective technique and craft—the skills he or she has learned
that one also wishes to master. That's why you show up at
this person's door. Not for their vision, because you're developing your own unique sense of how the world works. All
you need from a mentor are the tools.

23. The Wounds That Create Our Work

A psychological wound is helpful, if it can be kept in partial control, to keep the novelist driven.
　　　　　—John Gardner, *On Becoming a Novelist*

Does a writer need tragedy or loss as a motivation for doing his or her work? Is some sort of "wound" required in the life of the artist? We encounter this idea about creative people so often that it has the status of a cliché. For example, in *On Becoming a Novelist*, John Gardner writes:

> Some fatal childhood accident for which one feels responsible and can never fully forgive oneself; a sense that one never quite earned one's parents' love; shame about one's origins—belligerent defensive guilt about one's race or country upbringing or the physical handicaps of one's parents—or embarrassment about one's own physical appearance: all these are promising signs. It may or may not be true that happy, well-adjusted children can become great novelists, but insofar as guilt or shame bend the soul inward they are likely, under the right conditions (neither too little discomfort nor too much), to serve the writer's project.

With great sadness we understand why Gardner began the above paragraph with the example of a "fatal childhood accident for which one feels responsible and can never fully forgive oneself." When he was eleven years old, he was given the chore of returning a cultipacker to his parents' farm from a neighbor's place. His six-year-old brother, Gilbert, rode on the drawbar that linked the cultipacker to the tractor young JG was driving. Gilbert was killed when the tractor ran out of gas, the engine stopped with a jerk, and he was thrown to the ground in front of the cultipacker, which rolled over him. This terrible event haunted Gardner all his life, and he writes movingly about it in his short story "Redemption." His parents always insisted that he was not the cause of Gilbert's death, but JG apparently did not entirely believe that. There were times when he would be driving and the entire awful tableau would appear before his eyes again, right there superimposed on the windshield, and he would have to pull over to the side of the road until it passed.

I know—and you know, too—a great many stories about writers and artists, past and present, that contain some form of childhood trauma. An emptiness or scars or a wound so deep that the writer can find consolation for his (or her) grief and suffering only through the act of creating. While I don't have in my own life a single, painful event that was defining like JG's, I believe I understand what is common (and positive) throughout all the examples he presents: namely, that in order to create it is helpful if a person feels in some sense that he or she is a social outsider. The outsider is driven to question everything in the enveloping social world, to adopt a critical stance in the face of those things familiar and commonly accepted, to sometimes or often feel himself "at a distance" from things, and, most important of all, to carefully—sometimes obsessively—observe the behavior of others, which he can then describe in a work of fiction with detail and nuance.

At first glance, Gardner's thesis is compelling. (And it seems of a piece with William Gass's statement "I need hate to heat my art.") I can think of many examples to support it, from James Baldwin and Jean-Paul Sartre, who felt they were physically ugly, to the missing or absent fathers in the lives of August Wilson and Ralph Ellison, which literary scholars have identified as wounds that fueled their writing. But something feels slightly wrong with this picture. We need to examine it more closely.

In every example that Gardner gives, the writer is looking at himself through the eyes of others. He is defining his identity not simply by a loss or tragedy that took place but on the basis of what *others* think about it. He is not free. He is enslaved to their judgments, and one gets the feeling that he (or she) creates in order to change the real or imagined opinions of others about who and what he is. Indeed, the creative work that springs from the artist's wound and insecurity may well be a desperate bid for love. The protagonist in my story "The Sorcerer's Apprentice," Allan Jackson, faces a dilemma similar to this. He hungers to heal his family's racial and individual wounds through magic (art). In other words, he is *attached* to those wounds and also to his "identity" as a sorcerer, two ego-driven things that he eventually must learn to "let go", put another way, he must discover a new, different relationship with himself and his talent.

To a very large degree, then, Gardner is describing a form of neurosis. Notice how he says in a parenthetical aside that guilt or shame must involve "neither too little discomfort nor too much." Well, we know—and sadly—what happens to the writer or artist when there is "too much" guilt, shame, and discomfort. Or when he fails to keep his wounds under "partial control." Between or during periods of creativity, he or she may blunt that discomfort with drugs, alcohol, sexual adventures (and sometimes all three at once), or some other form of self-destructive addiction. One cannot help but feel that this description of the writer's wound as the basis for creativity is touching only on the surface of the malaise and not penetrating to its roots.

It is the wound, Gardner says, that makes the writer "driven." And there, my friends, resides the problem. This kind of writer knows no peace, only a chronic, free-floating sense of "discomfort." Unlike Gardner, I, being a Buddhist, don't see "identity" as any sort of enduring substance or essence. (And I greatly value *shanti*, or peace.) Our past is *gone* and can never be recovered—except through memory, which itself is a phenomenon that imaginatively plays with and reshapes over time our prior experiences. Furthermore, a Buddhist knows better than to shape his sense of self (when, in fact, there is no self) on the basis of other people's opinions.

Long ago, you may have done something that made you feel guilt or shame, but you are no longer that person *here* and *now*.

So I find myself taking the position that, yes, "happy, well-adjusted children" or adults *can* create great art, especially if they have a spiritual practice that keeps them on an even keel. Guilt and shame are not the *only* experiences that "bend the soul inward." Therefore, writers need not be attached to either their "wound" or the work it gives rise to. Instead, their work can spring from an abiding peace and feeling of thanksgiving; from the joy to be found in living mindfully and exercising their hard-won skills because exploring the inexhaustible pleasures of the ever-mysterious creative process feels so danged good.

24. The First Readers

I am more or less happy when being praised; not very comfortable when being abused; but I have moments of uneasiness when being explained.
— Arthur Balfour

Literature is strewn with the wreckage of men who have minded beyond reason the opinion of others.
— Virginia Woolf, *A Room of One's Own*

For forty-one years my wife has always been my first reader. I can trust that she will give me a "general reader's" reaction, and point out any typing errors I might have made.

The next readers are my agents of thirty-eight years, Anne and Georges Borchardt, who will either send the manuscript along to whatever editor commissioned it or find a home for it if it is a new work of fiction, and sometimes others in their office will read it, too. Between 1972 and 1982, I often passed my stories and novels by the late John Gardner for any helpful comments he might make (and knowing full well that our visions of life and literature differed in important ways). These days when I've finished a story, I often send it along to the literary scholars who have published articles and books about my work as well as the work of others. All are officers in the Charles Johnson Society at the American Literature

139

Association, and learned on matters pertaining to literature and culture, so I greatly value whatever they might have to say. I often share a brand-spanking-new work with friends who I think might find its subject of interest. Sometimes I'll send a new work to editors I know, ones I have a hunch might feel it is appropriate for their publication, and, if so, they can then contact my literary agents to work out a contract and payment.

I always take seriously any comments and suggestions I receive from all the aforementioned folks, and I think about them for a long time, because I want every work I create to be a gift for others.

But I should mention that I'm never ready to show anything I write to others until I've worked it over thoroughly and through many drafts in which I've revised each line until I can't revise it anymore, and not until I've considered every word choice dozens of times. The work is ready to show only after I convince myself that it reflects my best feelings, best thought, and best technique.

Writing screen- and teleplays is, of course, a different matter. For the most part, this is committee work (or collaborative work, if you prefer), and a writer is professionally obligated to respond to all the notes he receives from the producers of a particular show. He (or she) is part of a team, a "hired gun," so to speak. In one of his interviews, the playwright August Wilson talked about how when his first play was staged he had to get over a sense of ownership of the work, since the process of moving a play from the page to the stage involves contributions from many people. (Nevertheless, his ten plays clearly embody his own vision of black American life, since August had final approval on all changes.)

But for original, literary art, it should be obvious that too many "cooks" can muddle, dilute, or damage a story's coherence, clarity, and consistency, and sometimes move it too far away from a writer's intention. Seasoned, veteran artists know—and feel secure with—their own voices and visions of life and literature. What they believe and don't believe. What they want to say and how they think it is best to say it. Therefore, listening to "criticism" is not a problem, and is even quite interesting sometimes because a person's reactions to a creative work reveal as much about that person as they do about the work in question.

I believe James Baldwin addressed all these matters well in his essay "The New Lost Generation," published in the July 1961 issue of *Esquire*. This quote has been in my writer's workbooks for decades, patiently waiting to be deployed, so I'm happy for the opportunity to share it now. There, in that essay, Baldwin said, "A man is not a man until he's able and willing to accept his own vision of the world, no matter how radically this vision departs from that of others."

25. Writers and Editors

When I was twenty-four years old and writing *Faith and the Good Thing* with John Gardner looking over my shoulder, that writer/teacher gave me a bit of good advice regarding editors. He said before one turns in a manuscript to a publisher it should be as perfect as one can possibly make it. One should not rely on an editor to fix or repair anything in one's work. Furthermore, Gardner said, when an author becomes famous or well known, editors have a tendency not to touch his or her work. In other words, many successful, celebrity writers don't receive the benefits a good editor can provide.

Almost exactly a year later, I stumbled on an example of what Gardner possibly meant. I was at Viking Press, meeting with my editor, the late Alan Williams, for *Faith*. He told me Saul Bellow was in the building, so I asked if he'd introduce us. Alan walked me down the hallway to an empty conference room. At the end of a long table, Bellow was going over the galleys for his novel *Humboldt's Gift*. He'd flown in from Chicago and, with his coat off and shirtsleeves rolled up, was tearing the galleys apart, revising, intensely focused on those pages, already set in type. That impressed me. Bellow, a perfectionist, knew that this was absolutely the last chance he had to work on this novel before it was published and he had to finally let it go. Every contract in the early 1970s said that if an author changed more than 10 percent of his book when it was in the galley stage, he (the author) had to pay for those changes. (This was, of course, no problem for Bellow, who was a millionaire.) After that novel was published, Bellow was awarded the Nobel Prize for literature. Needless to say, I was impressed by his eleventh-hour revisions prior to his book's publication. So impressed that I took the opportunity in the months before *Faith and the Good Thing*, a novel written in nine months, was published to rewrite every descriptive passage to improve their language performance.

I believe Gardner was right. But I also feel that even the most accomplished writer can be helped by a second pair of good eyes—those of a learned editor steeped in literary culture like my editor for *Middle Passage*, the late Lee Goerner at Atheneum—looking over his (or her) work and catching small things the writer may have overlooked in the heat of the creative process.

26. On Reading

The man who does not read good books has no advantage over the man who cannot read them.

—Mark Twain

Read not to contradict and confute, nor to believe and take for granted, nor to find talk and discourse, but to weigh and consider.

—Sir Francis Bacon

The young . . . are today not enthusiastic . . . about books. They merely approve when books suit their politics. . . . I think it is a pity that they do not read for pleasure. They may presently find that an acquaintance with the great works of art and thought is their only real assurance against the increasing barbarism of our time.

—Edmund Wilson, *The Nation*, 1938

In one of our numerous e-mail exchanges E. Ethelbert Miller asked me: "In 'Night Hawks,' August Wilson mentions how black people didn't go see his plays. Do you feel sometimes that because of your style of writing your black reading audience might not be as large as you would like? I once coined the expression 'literary pork' to describe the type of books being consumed by black readers. Do you have any concern about this matter?"

I believe that Ethelbert and I both feel that Americans do not read enough. That includes black Americans. And when Americans *do* read, the works they select are seldom (if ever) intellectually challenging. "Literary pork" has always been—and most likely will always be—more popular than literary works that liberate our perception and challenge our presuppositions. One of my editors at the *New York Times Book Review* once put it to me this way: when motion pictures came along, literary culture had real competition, and by the time televisions were in most American homes, anything we might want to call literary culture was all but finished. We simply do not have a literary culture anymore—what we have instead is a widely shared pop culture provided by movies and television.

During one of my family's reunions in South Carolina, a young woman who married a relative of mine told me she "didn't like to read," but was making herself do so for the sake of her young son. In other words, to set a good example for him. And I remember, painfully, signing one of my books for a young black man after I gave a reading somewhere, and him saying to me, "I want to be a writer, but, you know, I don't like to read." When I did an event in Detroit a few years ago, the young black woman who introduced me said one of her friends told her she was just "giving up" on trying to read Charles Johnson because she had to look up too many words she didn't know. And who can forget Alice Walker's memorable reply to an interviewer who asked her what her relatives thought of her books? She said, "What makes you think they read?" I could give you a thousand examples of this kind of tragic intellectual laziness among American readers, black, white, and otherwise.

Like any writer, I've thought about this sad state of affairs since 1970, when I wrote my first novel. But my background is in philosophy, a field where the canonical texts (to say nothing of second- and third-tier works) are "invisible" to the vast majority of general readers. Since my undergraduate days, I've never read pop books or "literary pork" for pleasure. (And I just don't have the time or interest for watching 99 percent of what is on television.) Naturally, then, I've never had any interest in reading fluff. The thought of "dumbing down" what I write is something I'm simply congenitally unable to do, because I write, first and foremost, in order to discover and clarify things for myself. (And that's why I write a lot; there are countless subjects I want to explore in this vast, mysterious universe we inhabit.) If I couldn't do that, then I wouldn't write. From the beginning, rather than desiring a lot of readers, I instead just wanted to have smart ones (the kind of readers who appreciate philosophical explorations and literary invention), regardless of their race, ethnicity, religion, or background. That is, people who have a background in what Matthew Arnold referred to as "the best that has been known and said in the world." Those are my ideal readers, and have been since I first put pen to paper. But I've never been critical of writers who write for sales. They have to pay their bills and put their kids through college, too. If they can do that with "pork," then I say more power to them.

And for the sake of fairness, I should temper my usually dismissive remarks about literary "pork," or formulaic writing. In my teens I enjoyed, along with Marvel comics in the early 1960s, the easy art of Ian Fleming's James Bond novels, and the simple prose of John Steinbeck's *The Pearl* and *Of Mice and Men*. Like Nietzsche's, such works seduce us in our youth. But literary writers often feel a certain ambivalence toward the pulp writing that amused them in childhood, alternating between appreciation for its entertainment value and revulsion for its lack of depth. Even within the constraints of genre fiction (soap operas, graphic novels, space operas such as *Star Wars*) composed by talented writers one can occasionally find interesting ideas, memorable instances of characterization, and scenes that are moving. Certainly one often finds the virtues of plot and suspense. I've not forgotten that a sometimes scathing literary critic like John Gardner found, as a young man, something to praise in the novels of Mickey Spillane. At age nineteen, he kept a journal his sophomore year at DePauw University, transcribing his thoughts on what he was reading. In the facsimile reproduction of this 1952 journal, titled *Lies! Lies! Lies! A College Journal of John Gardner* (University of Rochester Libraries, 1999), he said of Spillane:

> By gol, the man is gifted. . . . Mickey boy can describe. Mickey boy can tell a story. (Granted, you've heard the story before.) . . . 1). He writes romances. His villans are all bad, or nearly. . . . I've never heard anybody who has read a Spillane book criticize it as I have here. That is to say, only those who have heard *about* him laugh at 'im. Correction: "Great" critics call him pulp. The same "great" critics called *The Naked & the Dead* the "greatest story to come out of the war." Bull, I say. Anyway Mickey is not so bad. As someone has said, he's "the highest of the lowest." To me, that's higher than the lowest of the highest.

Twenty-seven years later, Gardner was still wrestling with the difference between literary and pop fiction, or "pork," in his review of William Styron's *Sophie's Choice*, which is reprinted in *On Writers and Writing* (Addison-Wesley, 1994). In his review in the *New York Times Book Review* in 1979, Gardner was especially critical of *Sophie's Choice*. But two years later he'd changed his mind and wrote a statement he wanted to precede his review when it was included in *Critical Essays on William Styron*. Portions of that statement speak to a truth about the nature of literary form:

> I'm not sorry to have pointed out that *Sophie's Choice* transmutes the old "Southern Gothic" to a new universal gothic. . . . What I suggested, I'm sure, was that, in following the gothic formula, *Sophie's Choice* was a castle built on sand. What I now think is this: Most great American art is an elevation of trash. New Orleans tailgate funeral jazz was (or so I think on this particular Friday) aesthetically mediocre stuff, but out of it came the high art of Ellington, Gershwin and the rest. Out of trash films, including Disney at his worst, came writers ranging from William Gass and Ishmael Reed to (forgive the self-congratulation) myself. Styron did not simply use the gothic formulae, he transmuted them. What is wrong with gothics is not wrong with *Sophie's Choice*.

Ethelbert's Complaint (apologies to Philip Roth), as I will call it, is a lament heard throughout the community of American poets and writers of literary fiction. And it has *always* been with us—this feeling that we, as literary writers, are culturally going against the grain. Melville and his associates said the same thing about "literary pork" in their day. But there has always been an intimate connection between "high" and "low" art, the latter often inspiring the former. So I don't expect the popularity of works aimed at the lowest common denominator to change in our lifetime. And I'm profoundly thankful for the literate, intelligent readers I do have.

27. The Virtues of Journalism

If it bleeds, it leads.
—Old rule in journalism

I taught in a creative-writing program for thirty-three years. Obviously, I feel such programs have value. And the CW program at the University of Washington is especially distinguished (ranked once among the ten best out of nearly three hundred such programs in America), having on its faculty of about ten writers four who are MacArthur Fellows (Richard Kenney, Linda Bierds, and Heather McHugh and myself before we retired). Those writers, and their predecessors, are master teachers and have assisted countless students since creative-writing classes were started at UW shortly after World War II (I think the year was 1947) by the poet Theodore Roethke, winner of the Pulitzer Prize and two National Book Awards.

But I was never a product of writing programs. In terms of education, I was a product of journalism and philosophy. Historically, as I mentioned, creative-writing programs as we know them today did not exist until after World War II. And you find such programs only in America. Europeans I've spoken with find such classes to be baffling, like an oxymoron, insofar as the general notion across Europe is that literary creativity—such things as imagination, vision, and so on—cannot be taught. And I agree with that judgment. We can't teach imagination and vision. What creative-writing programs *do* teach when they are at their best is technique and aspects of craft. Also they place apprentice writers in direct contact with established ones, who can serve as their mentors. In those programs, many often have the chance to serve as editors on a literary journal, and to teach beginning poetry and fiction workshops. For their thesis, they must, ideally, produce a publishable work — a novel, collection of short stories, or volume of poetry. Again, in terms of the ideal, these theses would be sufficiently professional to secure the young writer an agent and hopefully his or her first book contract. Unfortunately, in too many cases that I've seen, what many MFA students mostly want after graduation is to get a tenured job teaching creative writing themselves, like their professors, rather than devoting their energies to writing and publishing prolifically.

So we have an important question before us: What would aspiring writers do if there were no creative-writing programs? I think they would learn the rudiments of their craft, the essentials, in the same place that writers in the twentieth century did before 1945. Namely, on newspapers. (Or perhaps now in our twenty-first-century equivalent to dead-tree journalism.) What writerly virtues does newspaper journalism teach that are of value to a fiction writer? In my professional experience, there are four:

(1) First, a writer for newspapers is conditioned from his or her first week on the job to write a lot and on many subjects. Typically, a journalist files three or four (and perhaps more) stories a week. You learn to write fast, and to not even *think* about that fact because it is a job requirement. In other words, you learn to make your first drafts clear and well structured. (Inverted Pyramid–style paragraphs for straight news stories, but more literary approaches are possible for features and longer-form journalism.) You learn that you can't afford to flinch before a writing assignment — a feature,

a news story, a weekly column, a book or movie review, an editorial, a lengthier op-ed opinion piece, an in-depth investigative series—and you certainly can't afford the luxury of that strange psychic condition called writer's block. (Try telling that to your editor: "Gee, boss, I've had writer's block for the last two weeks." Anyone who says that will soon be sending out his résumé and seeking employment elsewhere.)

(2) You learn to write for the broadest audience possible. An old rule of thumb was that news stories in the *New York Times* should be understandable by someone with a twelfth-grade education (for lesser papers the target was an eighth-grade education, but that rule was made back in the 1960s when our public school system was in much better shape than it is now). Once, we called newspapers the Fourth Estate, an essential feature of any democracy, because citizens who have the franchise, the right to vote, need reliable information to guide them in the decisions they make on election day. So being able to write for everyone—to communicate with everyone who can read—is something a journalist learns from day one on the job. And in the '60s when most major cities had two newspapers (often one that was liberal, the other conservative), a journalist typically paid attention to his paper's competition, that "other" newspaper in town to see what stories it might be covering that his own paper might have missed. Even now I'm still in the habit of reading every day two newspapers from different ends of the political spectrum.

(3) On newspapers, a writer learns to do research. He or she learns to ask the six most important storytelling questions: Who, What, When, Where, How, and Why? You have the library of news stories previously published by your paper—the morgue—to draw upon. But, more important, you learn how to interview people, to shut up and listen, and how to ask good questions. Remember: the quality of the answers we get in this life is based on the quality of the questions we ask.

(4) And, last, you learn not to see your prose (or copy) as sacred. Or carved in stone. What you write is just copy. It can always be improved by revision. When you're done writing, it goes directly across the room to your editor, who will delete, add to, and change what you wrote, sometimes in ways that might make you want to scream and pull out your hair, because your byline will *still* appear on that piece. In other words, being a staff writer for a newspaper teaches a writer humility. There is no place for prima donnas in the newsroom. Only for professionals who know how to get the job done *and* by or before its deadline.

These are not always the virtues (emphasized by the threat of being fired) that MFA students encounter in their more gentle, nurturing two-year programs. But the experience of writing for newspapers obviously served well generations of fiction writers from the late nineteenth century through the first half of the twentieth. I recommend this experience for apprentice literary writers today. Such an experience of writing every week from the trenches, so to speak, will only serve to make them better professionals when they turn to producing literature and working as writers who can take on *any* assignment that comes their way.

28. Practical Literary Advice

What a writer in our time has to do is write what hasn't been written or beat dead men at what they have done.

—Ernest Hemingway

In my classes I constantly emphasized the virtues I believed great writers brought to their creations. After one such mini-lecture twenty-five years ago that had me huffing and puffing for perhaps twenty minutes, a young woman raised her hand and said, "You know, I'm glad you told us that." I asked her why. Her reply was, "Because now I understand that I *don't* want to be a great writer. I just want to write a few stories and maybe get them published, and that's all."

I said, "Okay, that's fine," and I promised to do everything I could to help her achieve that goal. I relate this story because when we ask what advice we should give to young writers, or wonder what are the strategies for a "successful" literary career, it's important to first ask what a person *wants* from writing and publishing. Is it money? (If so, most apprentice writers would likely do better by going into real estate.) Is it about getting attention or creating poems, books, and stories as ornaments for their egos? (As a Buddhist, I have a few problems with that one.) Some people, like the young woman in my class, simply want to write for the sake of self-expression

153

and to have a little fun. Others want a career writing the kind of genre fiction they enjoy reading (romance novels, murder mysteries, fantasy, street lit, and so on). Still others hunger for what they consider to be "fame and fortune" and want their ephemeral personalities to leave an impression on the (equally ephemeral) contemporary literary scene.

There's nothing terribly wrong with any of these intentions. I'm not holding them up for ridicule—or at least not too high. The world of fiction writing is capacious enough to hold many different kinds of stories, many different kinds of writers. And offering "business" advice to writers so motivated is certainly easy enough: Get a good literary agent to handle your contracts, protect your interests and the rights to your material, and provide a statement of your yearly earnings for the IRS—unless you enjoy doing all that yourself. (With a good agent, you can forget about things like this and just create.) Make sure you pay your taxes. If you have one or more "big" years, make sure you set aside what you know you will owe Uncle Sam. (I've known way too many writers who after their fifteen minutes of fame didn't pay when they had a book that sold well, or somehow didn't notice that the MacArthur they received was taxable.) I would recommend getting a good financial advisor (or a team of advisors) who can wisely and carefully diversify a financial portfolio, and help you plan each year for your expenses, and for your retirement.

Get a lawyer to help you work out a will that explains in detail how you want your literary properties handled after you're gone (mine is fifty pages long, with much granularity of detail, and, even as I write this, I know it needs to be updated—all wills should be revisited every five to seven years or so). If you get rich, live like you're poor (but treat yourself to something you really want now and then, of course). Don't give up your day job, at least not immediately. I've always been fond of the image of the parsimonious company CEO who drives not a Lexus but an old beater and wears clothes off the rack. That's extreme, obviously, but you get what I mean: if you make a bundle, don't radically change your lifestyle. Just because you have a bestselling book (or a "hit record," as they say), there's no guarantee you will have another, especially if you're a literary artist and not writing formulaic fiction year after year. Let me say a bit more about that.

The commonplace advice offered above would cover (and skimmingly so) some aspects of the "business" side of any profession. But, in my view, a literary artist is not just producing over and over again a product or a commodity like toilet paper or a bar of soap. Movie people (and the salespeople in publishing) like to believe they can "target" audiences for a particular work. That's their job. Regardless of the merit of a work's content, they're supposed to think in terms of units sold and profits made or, as a Hollywood screenwriter friend of mine once put it, "asses in seats." But this may present a problem for literary writers who, from book to book, go wherever their robust imaginations take them. The audience for *Middle Passage* or the slave stories I wrote for *Soulcatcher* is—well, I guess it's generally people with some interest in the Peculiar Institution and matters related to the subject of race. I don't think that audience generally overlaps with readers of *Turning the Wheel: Essays on Buddhism and Writing* (or I'd wager at least not by much), nor should it overlap.

So this is for me a perennially interesting question, one wrestled with by every American writer I know about since the nineteenth century: art vs. commerce. From the time I first starting writing seriously and steadily when I was twenty-two years old, it seemed to me that the first thing *any* writer needed to determine before putting pen to paper was if he (or she) had something original and important to *say* or show us. A writer would be wise to ask, "What can I uniquely bring to the table that enriches literary culture? What is missing from our literature, and can I fill that lacuna?" James Weldon Johnson, Richard Wright, Zora Neale Hurston, and Ralph Ellison knew *exactly* what they were bringing to the table, what there was about their work that hitherto had never been seen in literary culture—and they produced the equivalent of literary manifestos or an *ars poetica* that made their artistic intentions clear. In my case, I wanted to contribute to a thematically and aesthetically expansive American philosophical fiction, especially in the area of black literature. August Wilson once asked me, "What makes a great writer?" I didn't hesitate, and replied, "A great vision." August nodded and thought about that. And then I added that good fiction sharpens our perception; great fiction *changes* it.

So before committing oneself to a lifetime of writing, I would suggest that every young literary fiction writer (and old ones, too) answer for themselves the questions Jean-Paul Sartre posed in *What Is Literature?*: "*Why* do I write? For whom do I write? What is writing? What do I hope to accomplish?" And I highly recommend that they consider first a statement from Saul Bellow's 1971 essay "Culture Now," which I placed before my students for three decades, and then August Wilson's "Four Rules" for writers.

Bellow wrote:

This society, like decadent Rome, is an amusement society. Art cannot and should not compete with amusement. It has business at the heart of humanity. The artist, as Collingwood tells us, must be a prophet, "not in the sense that he foretells things to come, but that he tells the audience, at the risk of their displeasure, the secrets of their own hearts." That is why he exists. He is a spokesman for his community. This account of the artist's business is old, much older than Collingwood, very old, but in modern times this truth, which we all feel, is seldom expressed. No community altogether knows its own heart, and by failing in this knowledge a community deceives itself on the one subject concerning which ignorance means death. The remedy is art itself. Art is the community's medicine for the worst disease of mind, the corruption of consciousness.

And here are August Wilson's "Four Rules":

1. There are no rules.
2. The first rule is wrong, so pay attention.
3. You *can't* write for an audience; the writer's first job is to *survive*. [Italics mine.]
4. You can make no mistakes, but anything you write can be made better.

The Writer as Teacher

29. The Literary Duet: Creative Writing and Critical Theory

Try to be one of the people on whom nothing is lost!
—Henry James, *The Art of Fiction*

We are all already contaminated by each other.
—Kwame Anthony Appiah,
In My Father's House

It is difficult for me to imagine a student in one of the nearly three hundred creative-writing programs in America (and we seem to have these only in America) not having the requirement of taking a certain number of literature courses. In those courses it is today nearly impossible to escape the interpretative or hermeneutic approaches we gather under the general term "critical theory."

As a philosophy graduate student in the early 1970s, I was immersed in works by Marxist-oriented authors considered to be the principal theorists of critical theory—the Frankfurt School philosophers (Marcuse, Adorno, Horkheimer, Habermas), Foucault, and Barthes. With my early emphasis on phenomenology and aesthetics, it was also inevitable that my literary studies would be influenced by not only the New Criticism of the 1940s and '50s but also structuralism, feminist theory, and, to a lesser extent, deconstruction. Every well-educated student of literature should be acquainted with these approaches.

Lately, or perhaps I should say since the 1980s, I find my interest moving toward certain aspects of critical race theory (CRT), specifically toward the area of "whiteness studies," that is, toward examinations that show us how "race" is historically constructed with the intention of perpetuating white supremacy and dominance. Very exciting work in this area is coming our way from the philosopher George Yancy. In the brilliant introduction to his book *Look, a White!: Philosophical Essays on Whiteness*, Dr. Yancy "flips the script" by inviting white readers to see themselves through the eyes of people of color, to see how "whiteness is the transcendent norm in terms of which they live their lives as persons" and how this recognition is so very *"threatening* to a white self and a white social system predicated upon a vicious lie that white is right—morally, epistemologically, and otherwise." *Look, a White!* is a book I recommend for all readers.

But whiteness studies are no longer limited to the world of the Academy. A recent article by Jen Graves in Seattle's *The Stranger*, entitled "Deeply Embarrassed White People Talk Awkwardly About Race," reveals how progressive whites are embracing the critical race theory critique of whiteness and attempting to address it through organizations such as the Coalition of Anti-Racist Whites (CARW), which meets every month at the downtown Y in Seattle. There, members confront what CARW's co-founder Scott Winn sees as the truth: "Whiteness is the center that goes unnamed and unstudied, which is one way that keeps us as white folks centered, normal, that which everything else is compared to—like the way we name race only when we're talking about a person of color. . . . We can name how some acts hurt people of color, but it's harder to talk about how they privilege white folks. . . .

I think many white people are integrationists in that 'beloved community' way, but integration usually means assimilation . . . as in, you've gotta act like us for this to work."

Graves says, "I grew up in a middle-class white suburban neighborhood. Although we never had a black family over for dinner, every house on our street hosted black men doing perp walks through our living rooms on the news. I didn't realize the contradiction until much later—that our seemingly all-white existence was predicated on keeping other people *other*." And in this lengthy article she shares Mab Segrest's observation that in terms of the lived experienced of whiteness, "Women are less white than men, gay people are less white than straight people, poor people less white than rich people, Jews than Christians, and so forth."

Needless to say, critical theory and critical race theory will not help an apprentice writer learn anything about *techne* or craft. Furthermore, during the creative process, which is one of discovery, theories and explanatory models should be set off to one side if a writer hopes to create on the basis of his or her own unique voice and vision. However, an acquaintance with critical theory and critical race theory fulfills Henry James's advice to a young writer (see epigraph), and in ways that James himself was probably unaware of. Every writer and student— and citizen—should know something about CRT. For the illusion of "race"—the racial *I*, self, or personal identity—and its everyday construction are difficult to thematize because they are presuppositions so ingrained in our cultural conditioning in the white West that they are almost invisible, and are as close to us in our daily lived experience as to go unnoticed like our breathing. The beauty of CRT investigations is that, at their best, they deconstruct such lies, illusions, and fantasies, forever changing—in a true phenomenological fashion (and one also compatible with Buddhist self-examinations)—the way we experience and create moment-by-moment our world.

30. The Creative-Writing Teacher as Soul Catcher

Most creative-writing teachers have had the experience of occasionally helping to produce, by accident, a pornographer.
—John Gardner, *The Art of Fiction*

It's not surprising if writers are often rather silly people, not always what we think of as intellectuals, and certainly not always freer of silliness or perversity than anyone else.
—Northrop Frye, *The Educated Imagination*

I'm all in favor of keeping dangerous weapons out of the hands of fools. Let's start with typewriters.
—Frank Lloyd Wright

During my thirty-plus years of teaching creative-writing students, graduate and undergraduate, I never told anyone that he or she lacked talent or imagination, or that they were wasting their time. Obviously, some did lack talent and imagination. Some were wasting their time. But in principle, I always considered it wrong to discourage anyone. Who can predict if the student performing poorly in a workshop today might in five or ten years blossom into a first-rate practitioner of memorable literary fiction? Or a bestselling writer of industrial fiction? And there is also this to say: even if such a young writer (and we all know that twentysomething young writers are notoriously lacking in the kind of worldly experience that is the basis for good storytelling) didn't one day write well, English professors console themselves, rightly or wrongly, with the hope that the young writer will emerge from a creative-writing workshop as a more critical reader, someone who better understands the creative process behind the works of writers they admire or love.

But having said that, I sometimes had in my classroom students whose sanity was questionable. Every creative-writing teacher I've known has had such students. For example, a former colleague at the University of Washington, the poet David Wagoner, tells of once having the serial killer Ted Bundy in one of his workshops. To paraphrase something once said by John Gardner, we sometimes run into a student who doesn't so much need to work on his or her craft but rather should first work on the condition of his or her *soul*.

On the first day of my classes, I told students that I cared less about *what* they wrote (that was up to them) than *how* they wrote it; *but* I also urged them to immediately begin reading Gardner's *The Art of Fiction*, where he states, "On reflection we see that the great writer's authority consists of two elements. The first we may call, loosely, his sane humanness; that is, his trustworthiness as a judge of things, a stability rooted in the sum of those complex qualities of his character and personality (wisdom, generosity, compassion, strength of will) to which we respond, as we respond to what is best in our friends, with instant recognition and admiration, saying, 'Yes, you're right, that's how it is!'" (The second element for JG is the writer's trust in his or her own aesthetic judgments and instincts.) I also made them reflect on these words from JG's literary manifesto, *On Moral Fiction*:

Clearly no absolute standard for sanity and stability exists, but rough estimates are possible. If a writer regularly scorns all life bitterly, scorning love, scorning loyalty, scorning decency (according to some standard)—or, to put it another way, if some writer's every remark strikes most or many readers as unfair, cruel, stupid, self-regarding, ignorant, or mad; if he has no good to say of anything or anyone except the character who seems to represent himself; if he can find no pleasure in what happy human beings have found good for centuries (children and dogs, God, peace, wealth, comfort, love, hope, and faith)—then it is safe to hazard that he has not made a serious effort to sympathize and understand. . . .

Despite all that emphasis on "moral fiction" in my workshops, I found it strange to discover how many of my bright male students were eager to write novels that were rather perverse variations on either Vladimir Nabokov's *Lolita* (grown men lusting in their stories after fifteen-year-old girls) or John Fowles's *The Collector* (grown men imprisoning young women for the purpose of sexual exploitation). Some wrote a combination of those story lines—Lolitas imprisoned for sexual exploitation. And there were always the young female students who wrote stories about saintly women who were driven to murder their abusive, despicable husbands, or arranged to have them beaten to a bloody pulp.

I remember one student in my last class before I retired had written a first-person story where the narrator/protagonist was a serial killer. Decades ago, when on a visit to the writing program at another university, I was forewarned about a white student I would have in my class who was convinced he was black. (Hip-hop "ghetto" black, mind you, not black like W. E. B. Du Bois or Gordon Parks.) In one of my own evening novel-writing classes at UW, a black male student in his forties, one who was trying to self-publish his fiction, decided he was dissatisfied with the descriptive passages in the work of his peers that particular night and, without warning, jumped up from his seat and began to demonstrate the ways different people, male and female, happy or sad, might walk across a room. (Another student chastised him for that impromptu, class-disrupting, theatrical outburst before I could get over my state of shock and speechlessness.) And it will probably take me several reincarnations to forget the young woman, a fundamentalist Christian, who wrote about gay gang rape in Sodom before the Almighty destroyed that Old Testament city.

In the mildest bad-case scenarios, a writing teacher must deal with students who rather than striving to simply tell a good, entertaining story instead use the occasion of their fiction to subject their teacher and fellow students to their personal problems and neuroses. (One of my former chairmen once told me he suspected creative-writing classes were so popular on campus because it is only in those classes that some students get the personal attention they crave. This isn't physics. These aren't lit courses where one is studying Shakespeare. Instead, they are the only classes on campus where the students' feelings and personalities are the subject matter.) But in a handful of cases the things I saw in student stories ranged from the eccentric to the bizarre to the borderline schizophrenic. When I was at UW it was briefly possible on the undergraduate level to weed out students who might potentially become a problem if a creative-writing professor was willing to request and read during, say winter term, samples of writing by students who wanted to enter his workshop scheduled for the spring. However, that practice soon ended, because students were afraid to submit a sample of their work and sought instead to get into sections of the class where the professor didn't ask to see their work before admitting them.

Is there a solution for any of this? If there is, I suspect it lies in the direction of the creative-writing teacher practicing patience and compassion toward his or her most troublesome students, taking them aside and in private explaining why some readers will find what they have put on the page to be offensive, and maybe even alarming. As much as some of us with a background in philosophy would like to believe that everyone is endowed with reason, the truth—at least in terms of my experience—is that everyone we meet is on a different level of emotional, intellectual, and moral maturity and development. Why should it be different in the classroom? And I'm always reminded of a telling statement once made by the spiritual teacher Eknath Easwaran: Each individual we meet during the course of our day is at any given moment most likely emerging *from* a state of depression, is already *in* a state of depression, or is just about to *enter* a state of depression. A sensitive teacher always keeps that in mind.

31. Writing and Teaching, or From Mr. Hyde to Dr. Jekyll

When I'm writing (or drawing), immersed in a fictional world that is unfolding before my eyes, I have to withdraw from the social world. The latter more or less ceases to exist for me. I become solitary. I go underground. The phone or doorbell ringing, the headlines of the day, stock market news, the weather and enveloping world of others and objects—all that recedes to the periphery of my consciousness. None of it moves from background to foreground unless it directly relates in some way to the story I'm trying to imagine with detail and precision. I can't "punch in" and write for just a few hours a day, then "punch out" as I did when I was a young journalist. I have to live and breathe the work all day long. When writing, I get silent. I don't want to talk, because all my language is going onto the page. I don't shave. I forget to eat and live on coffee, walk around the house in a sweatshirt and sweatpants, unmindful of the passage of time, making notes to myself for dialogue I suddenly hear in my head. I sometimes sacrifice my daily workouts. Personal hygiene suffers. (I have no idea how my family tolerates me during times I'm intensely at work.) I deliberately get sloppy and embrace chaos so that whatever I'm working on can have all the order I'm capable of mustering. I'm slow to return phone calls or answer e-mail or even look at the day's snail mail—

and have to apologize to others when I finally complete the work and break radio silence. I just work quietly, steadily, sleep when my brain needs rebooting (and sometimes find the work entering into my dreams), then go right back to work as soon as I wake up. I lose sense of time's passage. In effect, I leave the real world behind, because all my thought is directed toward the characters, their speech and actions and emotions; all my mental energy goes into writing and rewriting sentences in my head. All of it is devoted to problem solving. I'm living only for the "Aha!" moments of discovery and surprise as the story pushes ahead, one paragraph at a time.

I'm not the best person to be around when I'm working. I even doubt that I'm a "nice" person. For the sake of the characters, I have to sometimes let myself become emotionally raw and tender, irascible and "tetchy" and capable of saying and doing things (in my imagination) that I would never do or say in the real world. During these bouts of work I am not very attentive to others, what they are doing or their needs. Intellectually and imaginatively, I have to put myself at risk, be ready to throw out everything I think I know or believe about what writing should be for the sake of discovery; I have to drop all the masks we use in the social world, be vulnerable if a character is vulnerable, rude if a character is rude, intolerant if a character is intolerant, wicked if that character is wicked, and let the story lead me where it wants to go as I prayerfully move from one page to the next. To be frank, I love these periods of total immersion in work when I almost completely forget the external world and live entirely in one conjured from the imagination. When these periods are done, I usually treat myself to a good meal.

But in order to teach for thirty-three years I had to be exactly the *opposite* of what I've just described above. I had to make a 180-degree shift. From Mr. Hyde to Dr. Jekyll. From Dionysus to Apollo. From Cain to Abel. Because students and their needs *always* come first, they and they alone were at the center of my consciousness during class time and when I was on campus. As a teacher, I learned how to talk in other people's sleep (as the old joke goes), to fill an hour with speech if the students themselves were tight-lipped, and (sigh) to wear a suit if an occasion demanded that (and I've always hated wearing a suit and tying a little noose—oh, those are called ties—around my neck). To know which books and authors to point a student toward to help him or her with their own writing and research.

I learned how to exist completely as a public self, by which I mean that I left my personal life and needs outside the classroom door. (I never stepped on campus unless I first practiced meditation or mantra. Usually mantra.) For an artist or writer teaching is an invaluable experience (at least for the first five years or so), because one has to learn how to explain matters that remain on the level of the intuitive and instinctive when one is creating. (And when creating, one *has* to trust the intuition, the unconscious, the mysteries of the creative process itself.) You must learn how to explain what you and other writers do, *how* we do it, and make that doing something portable, i.e., understandable to both the tortoises and the hares in the classroom. Teaching makes you learn patience. And how to explain the same thing in several different ways. And over and over again, if necessary. If a student sent me an e-mail, I'd answer it immediately. I was greatly amused by a remark that my friend Nicholas Delbanco made when I visited his writing program at the University of Michigan. He said, "Ask him a twenty-second question and you get a twenty-minute answer." That's what three decades of teaching conditions an otherwise quiet and sometimes shy person to do. (But when I'm creating, my speech is spare, telegraphic, brief.)

Teaching required complete concentration on a roomful of others who were at first strangers then like new friends by the end of the second week, and an awareness of time so that a class would be well paced, giving each student exactly the right amount of room or freedom to express himself or herself, with all their wisdom and warts, knowing when to steer them back to the subject at hand if they started to wander, and provide structure that did not feel to the students to be in any way a constraint on their creativity. In other words, the classes I created had to have a clear form yet also be flexible based on individual student needs. Every student needed to feel respected, valued for his or her presence in the room. Don't let anyone tell you differently: Teaching was *work*. For me *and* my students. (See chapter 7, "A Boot Camp for Creative Writing.") I built my classes so that students couldn't hide; they had to work and be responsible to their professor and their peers in class. A teacher needs to be relaxed and at the same time as focused as a dog gnawing a bone. As the writer Jonathan Baumbach once said to me, it can be "emotionally exhausting."

After a class—especially one that ran for three hours—I never fooled myself into thinking I could easily go back to my own creative work, slipping effortlessly from such an outer-directed consciousness to an inner-directed one. The class, the students, thoughts of what I'd said or should have said (which I promised myself to say during the *next* class), ideas for how to make the next class even better, new handouts I wanted to photocopy and distribute to the class, would swirl through my head for the rest of the evening. (Now that I think about it, some of the same creative energy that went into a story also had to go into teaching ten weeks of classes.) A nap that night might reboot my brain so that I could resume my own work during the wee hours before dawn. Or sometimes it would have to wait until the next day after a good night's sleep.

The Writing Life
and the Duties of the Writer

32. The Art of Book Reviewing

Between 1977 and 2008, I published more than fifty book reviews in the *Los Angeles Times* (I was one of the handful of reviewers their editor convinced to do a book review every month starting in 1989); the *New York Times Book Review*; the *Washington Post Book World*; the *Chicago Tribune*; *Common Knowledge;* the London *Times*; the *Wall Street Journal*; the *American Book Review*; the *Seattle Weekly*; *Pacific Northwest*; *Tricycle: The Buddhist Review*; *Shambhala Sun*; and *Buddhadharma.*

I reviewed the work of many authors, among them Richard Wright, Raymond Roussel, Thomas McGuane, Cormac McCarthy, William Trevor, Barry Lopez, Toby Olson, Caryl Phillips, Chinua Achebe, Margaret Walker, Larry Neal, Wole Soyinka, Richard Rive, Stanley Crouch, Reginald McKnight, Shelby Steele, John Edgar Wideman, Gordon Parks, James H. Cone, Ben Okri, Kwame Anthony Appiah, John Updike, Gerald Early, Paul Theroux, Jerry Gafio Watts, Nelson George, Richard Ford, John Gardner, Dinesh D'Souza, Jim Crace, Albert Murray, Madison Smartt Bell, Jan Willis, William Styron, and angel Kyodo williams.

I decided that after more than fifty reviews, I could let reviewing become one of the things I'd done enough of and could finally "let go." (However, I keep getting pulled back when an editor puts an interesting text in front of me.) But why did I begin reviewing in the first place? The short answer is that I was eager to review books because I felt a serious writer has an obligation to respond to and be engaged with other contemporary authors during the moment they share in literary history.

Traditionally, and not that long ago, book reviewing was a literary art form in itself. (And not, as my daughter once said when she was a kid, "You're doing another book report, Dad?") Far from being like a high school book report, a well-done book review can be a thing of beauty as memorable as the book under review—and in some cases *more* engaging and memorable than the book being discussed. In the case of a writer like John Gardner, his reviews in the *New York Times Book Review* in the 1970s were often insightful "position papers" on some aspect of aesthetics (in his case, "moral fiction") inspired by whatever book he was discussing.

But I was not interested in my reviews being position papers. I preferred to restrict my taking of intellectual and artistic positions to my philosophical essays. Instead, and in a phenomenological spirit, the first thing I always did when approaching a book I had to review was "bracket" or set aside my own partisan, aesthetic positions, my personal feelings, and my notions of what a story or novel should be. That was something I hoped each text I reviewed would teach me anew. In other words, the first step was to get "me" out of the way. I sought to experience the work from within and in its *own* terms, and to let the text guide the aesthetic and cultural questions I would raise. I found that it was important to give readers as concise and accurate a summary of the book as possible, but in the case of a work of fiction never to reveal too much, because that would spoil the sense of surprise and discovery for them if they bought the book.

And, most important of all, I found it helpful to quote liberally and (when possible) at length from the book. Why? Well, because that way a reader could directly experience the work without me, the reviewer, as a middle term mediating (or standing in the way of) readers encountering the author's own thoughts and prose style. Personally, I might not like a particular book, and sometimes a reviewer is tempted to just throw up his hands and repeat the line attributed to Abraham Lincoln: "People who like this sort of thing will find this the sort of thing they like." But generosity in using quotations gives the reader a taste of the work's flavor, and lets him (or her) make up their own mind—they might just decide that they disagree with my judgment, if it was negative, and that this *is* a book they would find interesting.

In a word, I always tried to review the work of others with the kind of mindfulness, sympathy, compassion, and care that I hoped reviewers would bring to my own literary creations.

33. In Translation

According to my records, my work has been translated into Dutch, French, Italian, Japanese, Portuguese, Spanish, Greek, Chinese, South Korean, and Russian (with UK editions, too, of course). Predictably, the book most often translated is *Middle Passage.*

It's been said often, and rightly, that translation of literary work is impossible (the experience of the work as we move from one language to another can differ greatly) but necessary. I've seldom had the opportunity to work with foreign translators of my books. A couple of times, but not many. That fact led to some foreign editions that are, to put this politely, problematic. For example, in 1986 the French publisher Flammarion did a translation of my novel *Oxherding Tale* as *Le Conte du bouvier.* They brought me to Paris for a week of book promotion, and at that time I had the pleasure of speaking with the delightful young woman, Hélène Devaux-Minié, who did the translation. She explained to me that the novel's final chapter, entitled "*Moksha*," had given her much trouble. (In Sanskrit, it means "liberation from the cycle of birth and death, complete freedom, salvation.") She couldn't find, she said, that Hindu word in any of the French dictionaries she consulted. So instead for that chapter title she substituted the word *mokry*, which means "mockery." That word choice, sad to say, is entirely wrong and misleading.

Before I retired, I lined up on the bookshelves on one wall

in my office at the University of Washington all the American and foreign editions of my books (just in case we ever had a fire at our house and my other copies were destroyed). One was an Italian edition of *Oxherding Tale* entitled *Il Racconto del Mandriano*, published by Edizioni E/O in 1990. One day a student came into my office for a conference, sat down in a chair, and looked at that edition's cover. Then he asked, "Why is Langston Hughes on the cover of your book?"

Yes, that's right: Edizioni E/O had used as the novel's cover art an illustration based on a well-known photo of a young Langston Hughes. What were they thinking? Your guess is as good as mine. If only that publisher so far away had contacted me about its plans for the cover! But such was not the case. Moral of the story? If you *can* work with a foreign publisher and translator for one of your titles, I highly recommend that you do so.

34. On Screenwriting

Unlike the unhappy screenwriter in my story "Moving Pictures," I never abandoned literary fiction for the lure of Hollywood. However, over some twenty years I wrote twenty screen- and teleplays for PBS (among them *Charlie Smith and the Fritter Tree* in 1978, which was about the oldest living American; and *Booker*, which won a 1985 Writers Guild Award for best script in the category of children's television, and many other awards); screenplays for Tri-Star, Interscope, Columbia, and Showtime; and in 1981 I worked as one of two writer-producers for the second season of the PBS dramatic series *Up and Coming* (a kind of forerunner to *The Cosby Show*, about a black family's trials and tribulations). I was the writer-in-residence for WGBH's New Television Workshop (1977–78), and in 1992 hosted a four-part KCTS (Seattle) series, "Charles Johnson: Words with Writers," a segment of the hour-long show *Inside*. (The authors I interviewed were Tom Robbins, August Wilson, Anne Rule, and David Wagoner.) Being a college professor, I never felt the need to become a full-time player in film or television, but the work I did was enough for me to become "vested," that is, to qualify for early retirement and receive a monthly pension check from the Producer-Writers Guild with, of course, the possibility of working again as a screenwriter if something comes along that interests me.

Many of the workers I knew in the filmmaking business

came from film school, places like Cal Arts, where they learned the technical side of their craft well. But filmmakers frequently call upon the services of accomplished novelists and short-story writers because they are strongly grounded in two things important for any story, regardless of its medium: well-developed characters and structure (plot).

Obviously, filmmakers learn much from literary artists. For example, when the actor Kirk Douglas published his second book, a potboiler called *Dance with the Devil*, he told an interviewer, "I feel a novel is really an extension of acting. When you're writing, you're playing all the parts: the women, the children, old men, young men. And it's a big ego trip because you have control of their destinies."

Just as filmmakers benefit from a novelist's particular skills, so, too, the literary writer can more finely hone his (or her) craft through screenwriting, where everything in a story must be dramatized and concretely realized as a scene actors can actually perform (during a read-through they *will* goof on written lines that violate the authenticity of real speech). The novelist writing for film is reminded that in a script there is a front story (plot) and a back story (situation.) In a novel or a short story, one can rely on narrative summary (telling, not showing) and the poetic possibilities of language to hold a reader's interest. Not so in a screenplay or teleplay. If one is, for example, adapting a novel for the screen (or, if you like, the stage), all those places where the novelist's mind went on autopilot, failing to "show and not tell," where he or she fell back on narrative summary or an entertaining voice or his or her talent for lyricism and left an action ambiguous or only suggested—well, *those* are precisely the places where a screenwriter must struggle to create a vivid scene, dramatic or otherwise. Thus, some novels and stories with minimal plot (but lots of dazzling language performance) are difficult to successfully adapt as films. Imagine the challenge a screenwriter would have with Djuna Barnes's 1936 classic *Night-wood*.

After my work on a script was done, I'd often hang around the set watching the actors and director work, and doing a last-minute rewrite if that was called for.

Watching the directors on various productions was always fascinating because of all the things they had to consider—how entrances and exits would be made; on what line (or part of a line) an actor will begin to cross the room, or turn to face another actor; the delicate and rapid interplay of shots from close-ups to two-shots to wider shots; the stress placed on a particular line that will trigger the reaction from other characters. Was this useful, I wondered, for fiction? Would it help a writer to organize a literary scene by walking through it himself, taking the roles of the characters at each particular moment? Certainly in our everyday lives we pay no attention to timing, the delivery of our lines (what we say to one another and how), unless perhaps we have a theatrical background or are very self-conscious (or crazy). But in film and television, I saw, everything was beautifully structured and thought through—the interplay of speech and gesture and body movement to maximize the desired effect on an audience.

For me, the payoff from writing screenplays probably came in *Middle Passage*, a novel that moves at a fast clip from one dramatic (or comic) scene to another (some people have told me they read the novel in one sitting), with narration used basically as a bridge (a poetic one, I hope) between scenes (of action and dialogue) and to prepare for them. Some writers I know, like my friend the sci-fi writer Steven Barnes, with whom I co-wrote a tale called "4189" in *The Burning Maiden* anthology, first compose their novels *as* screenplays in order to carefully lay out the dramatic structure, then in later drafts add narration (telling), with all its rich possibilities.

For those interested in a brilliant and very accessible explanation of how great films are examples of superb storytelling, I suggest two books by Brian McDonald, *Invisible Ink: A Practical Guide to Building Stories That Resonate* and *The Golden Theme: How to Make Your Writing Appeal to the Highest Common Denominator*. McDonald has taught his story-structure seminars at Pixar, Disney Feature Animation, and Lucasfilm's ILM. He is an award-winning director/writer who has written comic books and graphic novels, and for A&E's *Hoarders*, and has directed spots for Visa. His highly entertaining film *White Face*, which imagines what it would be like if circus clowns were a separate race, has run on HBO and Cinemax, and is used nationwide by corporations as a tool for diversity training. In a word, Brian McDonald is a master teacher whose every word on screenwriting you can trust.

35. Editing and Small Presses

Some editors are failed writers, but so are most writers.
—T. S. Eliot

During the years 1978–98, I served as the first fiction editor for the *Seattle Review*. Over the course of those two decades I had the pleasure of seeing that literary journal publish many writers, ranging from those who at the time were established and even famous (Joyce Carol Oates, John Gardner, Nicholas Delbanco) to the "emerging" (Daniel Orozco) and the new (David Guterson). As one might guess, the real joy in selecting fiction for the *Review* came from discovering memorable stories from new writers whose work, given the always stiff competition for publication in commercial or mass-market magazines, might not have found a home. (Early in my own life, many of my stories now frequently reprinted and anthologized appeared originally in literary journals such as *Indiana Review*, *Antaeus*, *MSS*, *Callaloo*, *North American Review*, *Mother Jones*, and *Choice*.) Historically, it is there, in the thousands of literary magazines in America, that many destined to become our finest writers first see their work in print.

It has always seemed to me that a "well-rounded" life as a writer involves not simply producing one's own creative work but also serving whenever possible what we call the larger literary culture in this country. In other words, helping others who do work we admire to find an audience. I count myself as fortunate in having had many opportunities to serve talented writers of every race, gender, and cultural background at each stage of the creative process—first by offering rigorous literary art instruction in my beginning, intermediate, advanced, and graduate classes at the University of Washington (and elsewhere) for thirty-three years; then providing many people with their first publication in the *Seattle Review* for twenty years (some of those stories later received awards); and writing endorsements (blurbs) for their earlier and later books (these fill two and a half bookshelves in my library); and finally by serving as a fiction judge given the privilege of honoring their work with national literary prizes, grants, and fellowships.

The spiritual principle here is that whatever we want for ourselves we should also want for others. Or, as Martin Luther King, Jr., said in "The Three Dimensions of a Complete Life," the sermon he felt captured his vision best, the second dimension for completion and fulfillment in life is learning "that there is nothing greater than to do something for others." Or put it this way: If you want to be happy, first try to make someone else happy. Publishing other writers is one small way of achieving that goal.

Philosophy and the Writer

36. Writing Well Is Thinking Well

The statement I often repeat, "Writing well is the same thing as thinking well," can be linked to that old chestnut, "Ninety percent of good writing is rewriting." This is not to say that "first thought" on a subject is not useful (or "First thought is best thought," as Allen Ginsberg put it). My writer's notebooks are filled with "first thought" lines that came to me unbidden at various times during the day, which I jotted down because they were perfect or nearly perfect in the form they originally took.

But the best writing on the level of the sentence (as well as larger structures such as plot and character detail) is usually twentieth or one hundredth thought. Personally, I don't feel we should burden people by showing them our first drafts; rather, what we share should be at least a third draft. With the first draft, every page is like a prayer—in that draft we put something on paper just to determine whether it is worth our continuing to work on it (or at least continuing in that particular way). Why? Because a writer strives for concrete details. People are generally vague and avoid being specific or precise because they hope to escape scrutiny. They think that if they are vague in details, like the onetime presidential candidate Herman Cain or Donald Trump, no one will be able to pin them down. Art is just the opposite of that: it hungers for and seeks specificity.

Obviously, this meticulous attention, this meditation on detail, requires time. And great patience. The creative process requires time to consider dozens of alternatives for a single word. Time to experiment with the form of a sentence, shaping it as one might a thing of plastic or clay. We come to understand that, unlike automatic writing or certain kinds of Zen art produced in a single stroke without one's brush or pen leaving the paper, creating a work of art is generally a process of thinking and rethinking everything that appears in one's first draft.

One of my former editors at the *New York Times Book Review* put it this way: a masterpiece is a story that does *not* need to be rewritten. When we consider such a work, we find it difficult to think of it being otherwise than it is, in all its parts and pieces, because they reinforce one another so well, creating a work that feels organic, whole. The reason for that is because the writer (or artist) is way ahead of the reader insofar as he or she has imaginatively, intellectually, and emotionally considered every possible variation on character and event, every possible word choice, and why the words finally selected are logically and necessarily the best words at this moment in the story.

In one of my writer's notebooks, I reminded myself, "The beauty and basic soundness of craftsmanship (*techne*) is a form of truth. Its very well-made quality is truth. Shoddiness, slipshod work of inferior quality—reflecting errors, haste, and indifference—is the absence of truth, the denial of truth."

"Thinking well" when writing also means that the writer considers the impact, consequence, or possible reaction readers might have for each and every word in his (or her) work, for every speech and action in a story. You must relentlessly ask questions about every decision you make and how it will be received or experienced. Is a statement accurate? Have you checked and double-checked every fact? Is a sentence, image, or word in poor taste? None of this means that you censor yourself. (There is no way that a writer can be all things to all people or satisfy everyone. As Milan Kundera once said, only kitsch is art that has a "desire to please at any cost.") But it does mean that you take into account the possibility that you might unintentionally offend or hurt a reader by one of your decisions—and, if one is a moral writer, you choose *not* to do that. And it also means that after thinking about a decision hundreds of times, you decide to stick by it (if you love what's on the paper and feel it is right and proper) even if it ruffles a few feathers.

In every sense, then, writing *is* thinking. Thinking with certain tools specific to the storytelling process, but thinking nevertheless. And the rules of rigorous thinking (like logic) apply to storytelling as much as they do to expository writing or any form of speech or expression.

37. The Writer and Philosophy

Philosophy: (Gr. philein, to love—sophia, wisdom)
—Dagobert D. Runes,
The Dictionary of Philosophy

To philosophize is not to examine the things of which one is conscious, but rather to examine the very consciousness one has of things—the mode of being which things have when we are conscious of them. Thus, to say that philosophy must examine the consciousness of things is but another way of saying that it should examine the appearance of things, i.e., the being they have when they appear.
—Quentin Lauer, *Phenomenology:
Its Genesis and Prospect*

I do not wish to argue that a novelist or any writer should be a trained philosopher. But I *will* say categorically that I believe *any*one in the Western world who wishes to be a serious writer (or thinker) should be acquainted with the geography of Western intellectual history (as trained philosophers are).

The basis for this argument is a no-brainer. Writing does not take place in a historical vacuum. If one hopes to make an artistic or intellectual contribution to Western literature, it follows that one should know what has come before, that is, what one is making a contribution *to*, and what our predecessors have thought and achieved. That is our intellectual inheritance. Yet it is important to remember, despite the sense and meaning we have received from our predecessors and ancestors, that the philosopher remains a perpetual beginner who takes for granted nothing that men and women, learned or otherwise, believe they know, as Maurice Merleau-Ponty makes clear in *The Phenomenology of Perception*. The philosopher doesn't spend his or her time reflecting on a preexisting truth, but instead, like the artist, is engaged in the act of bringing truth into being.

Even if a fiction writer limits himself just to reading "stories" (and I can't imagine why someone would do that, since our greatest literary predecessors didn't), he will find that they plunge him into the history of ideas. Can one fully comprehend and appreciate Voltaire's *Candide* with no knowledge of Gottfried Leibniz; or John Gardner's *Grendel* and Richard Wright's *The Outsider* and "The Man Who Lived Underground" without some understanding of existentialism; or even Charles Olson's poetry with no knowledge of Alfred North Whitehead's "process philosophy"? So, no, I don't see fiction as being merely entertainment, especially philosophical fiction, which one might say is equivalent to what physicists call a "thought experiment." A serious work is also an invitation to think critically and experience the world with different eyes. And every story is a transcendental object, i.e., an aesthetic object brought into being (our experience) by sustained acts of consciousness. (See Mikel Dufrenne's magisterial *The Phenomenology of Aesthetic Experience* for more on this.)

I will cop to the fact that over the last forty years I've known a great many fiction writers who were egotists, loved to hear the sound of their own voice *only*, seemed to feel the cosmos rotated around their wonderful selves, and, like far too many Americans, didn't feel they had any need for intellectual self-improvement. Perhaps that comes with the territory of being a writer—a large ego in order to sustain oneself during the vicissitudes in one's career. But there is a truly annoying arrogance and naïveté involved when someone says, usually defensively and in an effort to protect his ego, that he doesn't need to know what our ancestors and contemporaries of all races, backgrounds, and cultural orientations have thought and felt. Or when someone believes that his limited personal experience during eighty or ninety years of living (which is preposterously brief, given the 4.5-billion-year history of the Earth) can take the place of two or three millennia of intellectual or philosophical discourse.

Furthermore, most of the ideas expressed by writers today are not new. Far too many writers are simply unaware that an idea they believe is original was actually thought and expressed—and presented with eloquence and sophistication—more than two thousand years before they were born. Writing well is thinking well. That necessarily involves knowing—and caring about—the best thoughts of others. The kind of writer I'm talking about needs not just "personal experience" but also years of systematic study and, most important of all, a sense of humility: that is, the knowledge that better minds than his own have probably addressed the problem or experience or question that he is wrestling with today, and done so memorably, with sophistication and subtlety. You don't need a PhD in philosophy, I'm saying, to write well. But you *do* need to have an open, inquisitive mind, one eager to learn what others—as many intelligent others as possible—have reported down through the ages on the very human question you are trying to clarify. And the beauty of philosophy, the mother of all intellectual disciplines, is that it once contained or touched upon all the fields of investigation that we work in today. Physics did not separate itself from philosophy until the seventeenth century; chemistry in the eighteenth; biology in the nineteenth; and psychology in the twentieth. But the questions still central to the domain of philosophy are ones that remain crucial for our experience—for example, the questions of justice, morality, free will, and knowledge.

When thinking about this matter, I always find myself remembering Julius Lester's essay collection *Falling Pieces of the Broken Sky* (1990), and especially what he wisely says in one lovely piece, entitled "The Cultural Canon." Let's listen to *his* historically important voice for a moment:

> The function of education is not to confirm us in who we are; it is to introduce us to all that we are not. Education should overwhelm us to such an extent that we will never again assume that our experience as individuals or as part of a collective can be equated with human experience. In other words, education should impress us with how vast creation is and how small we are in the midst of it; and in the acceptance of that is the beginning of wisdom.
>
> My education did not confirm me as a black man; it confirmed me as one who had the same questions as Plato and Aristotle. And my education told me that as a black person, it was not only right to ask those questions, it was even okay to put forward my own answers and stand them next to those of Plato and Aristotle. The cultural canon was presented to me in such a way that I was thrust into that vast and complex mystery which life is; and I graduated from college with an intense and passionate curiosity, which led me to study that which my formal education had omitted—namely, black history and literature and women's history and much, much more.

It is the function of education to introduce the student to the terrifying unknown and provide not only the intellectual skills to make known the unknown but the emotional stability to withstand the terror when the unknown cannot be made known. Such an experience gives the student the self-confidence to go forth and face that mystery which lies at the core of each of us: Who am I?

38. Fiction and the Liberation
of Perception

We have never lived enough. Our experience is, without fiction, too confined and too parochial.
　　　　—Martha Nussbaum, "Love's Knowledge"

So long as art is identified with amusement, criticism is impossible.
　　　　—R. G. Collingwood, *The Principles of Art*

The writing of fiction is a mode of thought because by imitating we come to understand the thing imitated.
　　　　—John Gardner, *On Moral Fiction*

In an article published thirty-one years ago in *Obsidian*, "Philosophy and Black Fiction" (1980), I argued that "the final concern of serious fiction is the liberation of perception." I also stated in that article, "Our experience as black men and women completely outstrips our perception—black life is ambiguous and a kaleidoscope of meanings rich, multi-sided, and what the authentic black writer does is despoil meaning to pin down the freshest interpretation given to him. This is genuine fiction. It is also hermeneutic philosophy, in the sense that the writer is an archaeologist probing the Real for veiled sense."

A third of a century later, it still seems to me that the greatest literary art has an epistemological mission. By now this position should be uncontroversial. I'm not talking about mere "entertainment" (though great fiction certainly entertains), or the garden-variety novel, escapist literature, or fiction as a form of recreation. Rather, I am referring to fiction (and all Saying and Showing) that deepens our knowledge and refines our ways of seeing and experiencing the world.

In her often-cited work "Love's Knowledge" (1990), the philosopher Martha Nussbaum says, "In a sense Proust is right to see the literary text as an 'optical instrument' through which the reader becomes a reader of his or her own heart." A similar understanding of fiction is found in William Faulkner's Nobel Prize acceptance speech, and in Saul Bellow's essay "Culture Now." Nussbaum continues, saying, "One obvious answer was suggested by Aristotle: we have never lived enough. Our experience is, without fiction, too confined and too parochial. . . .

"All living is interpreting; all action requires seeing the world *as* something. So, in this sense, no life is 'raw.' . . ." (In other words, our experience is already *cooked* by our conditioning, education, intentionality, prejudices, assumptions, and presuppositions.) "The point," says Nussbaum, "is that in the activity of literary imagining we are led to imagine and describe with greater precision, focusing our attention on each word, feeling each event more keenly—whereas much of actual life goes by without that heightened awareness, and is thus, in a sense, not fully or thoroughly lived."

In other words, we betray the artwork if our attention is too brief. An insight similar to Nussbaum's can be found in Irwin Edman's *Arts and the Man: A Short Introduction to Aesthetics*:

The novelist is, in one sense, your true philosopher. For any marshaling of people into a story implies a conception of fate and a philosophy of nature. The least obviously philosophical of novelists, in the choice he makes of events, in the construction he makes of circumstances, indicates and implies what the world, his world, is like. Where novelists, like some of those in our own day, Hardy and Anatole France and Thomas Mann, are philosophers, they are so in a more rich and living sense than the philosophers of the academy. They imply themselves or express through their characters a total appraisal of existence. They document their estimates with the whole panorama of human experience. They not only judge but create a world. It is difficult to find in current philosophy a universe more complete and comprehensive than that of a novelist whose mind has ranged over eternity and whose eyes and imagination have traveled widely in time.

John Gardner echoes this understanding in *On Moral Fiction*. There, he states, "In fiction we stand back, weigh things as we do not have time to do in life; and the effect of great fiction is to temper real experience, modify prejudice, humanize. . . . When the writer accepts unquestioningly someone else's formulation of how and why people behave, he is not thinking but dramatizing some other man's theory: that of Freud, Adler, Laing, or whomever. But the final judgment must come from the writer's imagination."

And that imagination, according to Percy Shelley in "A Defense of Poetry," is "the great instrument of moral good." Shelley argues, "Poetry defeats the curse which binds us to be subjected to the accident of surrounding impressions . . . It makes us the inhabitants of a world to which the familiar is in chaos. It reproduces the common universe of which we are portions and percipients, and it purges from our inward sight the film of familiarity which obscures from us the wonder of our being."

It should be obvious that such perception-liberating art is the antithesis of ideology, clichéd thinking, kitsch, the unimaginative, and works that do no more than recycle pre-established or secondhand meanings and interpretations of our experience. Real fiction makes the familiar *un*familiar. It shakes up calcified ways of seeing. It activates in us a Beginner's Mind, as Buddhists would say. And we can never again think of a subject, event or experience without recalling the work of art—the gift—that caused scales to fall away from our eyes.

39. New Fiction Novelists

In 1974, the same year I published *Faith and the Good Thing*, Joe David Bellamy published a collection of interviews entitled *The New Fiction* (University of Illinois Press). Those young (at the time) writers he interviewed were John Barth, Joyce Carol Oates, William H. Gass, Donald Barthelme, Ronald Sukenick, Tom Wolfe, John Hawkes, Susan Sontag, Ishmael Reed, Jerzy Kosinski, John Gardner, and Kurt Vonnegut, Jr. Quite a diverse list, wouldn't you say? Everything from traditionalists to surfictionists, metafictionists, and satirists.

In his preface, Bellamy said:

Whether the new fiction of the last decade represents a "breakthrough" into fruitful new vistas or the "exhaustion" of a decadent, spent art form, it is, at least, drastically different from the fiction written immediately before by the great American modernists (as they have come to be called) and is based apparently upon totally revised assumptions about the nature and purpose of art. . . . Concurrent with the outpouring of some remarkable innovative fiction during this period, of course, numbers of writers continued to work skillfully in traditional modes, relying basically on nineteenth-century conventions for journalistic—or other nonfictional—purposes. In other words, amazing, sweeping, and unanticipated as its appearance has proven to be, the new American fiction is by no means monolithic, ubiquitous, or the result of any conspiracy, though it is no less amazing for that.

In constructing his definition of the "new fiction," Bellamy contrasts it to the literary naturalism that arose in the late nineteenth century. Think of Stephen Crane's "The Open Boat" (1897) and "Maggie: A Girl of the Streets" (1893), a work so scandalously "realistic" in depicting the protagonist's sordid world that Crane had to publish it himself and only one bookseller carried it. Crane was known for journalistic authenticity—he knew a "madam" of a brothel, and he himself was lost in an open boat, but apparently didn't need to go to war in order to write *The Red Badge of Courage*. I think at this juncture we need to distinguish between "realism" and "naturalism." You find the former in all sorts of literary traditions dating back thousands of years, even in fantasy writing where, say, a knight's shield may be described with great fidelity to detail and "realism" before he fights a dragon.

But literary naturalism is, like philosophical naturalism, a specific interpretation of how the world works, physically and psychologically, one that by necessity had to be revised on the basis of new evidence. It arose as a literary movement between the 1880s and 1940, attempting to explain "scientifically" the underlying social and environmental forces that shaped a person or a character, excluding anything regarded as spiritual or supernatural. In an important development in philosophy coeval with the rise of literary naturalism, many thinkers saw the flaws and dangers in the scientific sources this literary movement drew from. For example, the phenomenologist Edmund Husserl critiqued the "Natural Attitude" (*Einstellung*) as being the everyday unreflective attitude of naïve belief in the existence of the world, a rationalism that either presupposes abstract principles or the uncriticized results of science. This is what we call scientism. Most mimetic fiction even today, I would say, is written from the standpoint of the Natural Attitude — an attitude, as the Buddhist teacher Bhikkhu Bodhi tells us, plastered over with layers of conceptual paint (assumptions, presuppositions) that lacks the radical empiricism involved in "taking stock" of each and every one of our experiences.

Naturalism as a literary movement, then, is problematic because of the presuppositions in its very materialistic and at times deterministic model of Nature, which generally is Newtonian physics (the classical model), which collapsed by the mid-twentieth century due to the discoveries of relativity theory and quantum mechanics. Alfred North Whitehead had published *Process and Reality* (1929), a major work of "process philosophy" that attempted to account metaphysically for the discoveries of the new physics. Interesting, too, is how Whitehead's work offers a defense of theism, though his God has no resemblance to that of traditional religions. (And some commentators find parallels with Buddhist *abhidharma* or metaphysical writings in his work.) Even earlier, William James in his Gifford Lectures delivered at the University of Edinburgh (1901–02), which became *The Varieties of Religious Experience: A Study in Human Nature*, chastised the scientists in his audience for dismissing the value of religion.

The New Fiction that Bellamy sees emerging in the 1960s and early '70s is a fiction sensitive to the philosophical and scientific naïveté in some exhausted, "decadent, spent" modernist fiction. As so often happens in literary history, it was a reaction by a new generation of American writers to the rules and reasoning they inherited from their predecessors (just as Sherwood Anderson, D. H. Lawrence, and others reacted against the definitions of the modern short story as defined by Poe, O. Henry, and the critic Brander Matthews) and the unquestioned dominance of literary naturalism for three generations. It was sensitive to other, non-Western cultures and how they described reality. It questioned the very *foundations* of the kind of fiction written between the 1880s and 1940s, even its writerly techniques, which embodied an uncritical *weltanschauung*. Many works by these authors were self-referential or deliberately self-conscious, shattering the illusion that stories were anything other than a linguistic game; some of the writers were antirealists (in the philosophical sense of that term), acknowledging that a work of fiction is always a deliberately constructed artifice, never a mirror held up to reality. (See William H. Gass's brilliant essays on writing in *Fiction and the Figures of Life*.) How could it not be thus, when in so many ways our understanding of the enveloping physical universe was so radically transformed? The response of, say, a John Gardner was genre-bending and to sometimes return to the prenaturalistic tale-telling tradition.

Personally, I have the same great affection for the tale—an obvious fabulation—as a literary form in which aspects of spirituality can be explored without having to justify the presence of the life of the spirit in a story. I feel the same way about science fiction, first because it can address cutting-edge scientific discoveries, and second because sci-fi over the course of its long history often assumes the conventions of the tale. But when a story demands a naturalistic approach (which most readers are conditioned to prefer—I'm thinking of readers who say tedious and tiring things like "Did that really happen? Your character used drugs—do *you* use drugs?"), like the ones in *Soulcatcher and Other Stories*, I render the fiction in those familiar naturalistic terms in that tradition.

40. Science Fiction and
the Philosophical Novel

Back in the 1980s, the science fiction writer and feminist Joanna Russ (I think her best-known book is *The Female Man*), who was also good friends with the magisterial sci-fi writer Samuel R. Delany (*Dhalgren* and *Trouble on Triton: An Ambiguous Heterotopia*), was my colleague at the University of Washington. I interviewed them together for an issue of the *Seattle Review*. Both are pioneers of the "New Wave" of science fiction that emerged in the early 1970s, a science fiction that grappled with social issues and elevated the craft of good writing (strong characters, poetic, lyrical prose) in this genre. In that interview, Russ remarked that a woman living somewhere in America, perhaps in a very provincial, rural setting, once said that what she enjoyed most about science fiction was the landscapes. They helped her imagine, she said, a world quite different from the one in which she was living.

Russ, I should add, was both brilliant and prolific. I know because I wrote the report for her promotion to full professor at the University of Washington, and often gave her patriarchy-smashing essay "What Can a Heroine Do? Or Why Women Can't Write" to my students. Also, I've long pondered her casual remark one day that the dramatic plot strategy we call traditional "rising conflict or tension to resolution" suspiciously resembles the pattern of the male orgasm.

At any rate, I've always liked her statement about land-scapes, because it says science fiction (like philosophy) has the power to shake up our presuppositions, our assumptions, our social and cultural conditioning, our prejudices, and nudge us to imagine *What if?* To imagine things differently is the first step in changing the world as it is given to us. It is, in fact, the first step toward freedom.

In one of his lectures, Robert Thurman, a Buddhist scholar, disciple of the Dalai Lama, and director of Tibet House in New York City (and also father of the actor Uma Thurman), said that Buddhists are naturally fans of science fiction. Why? Once again, because philosophy, Buddhism, and science fic-tion at their best (as well as science itself) challenge our views and transform our perception. Philosophy does it through the rigor of reasoning and logic; science fiction does it by dra-matizing the possible, especially the possible based on either scientific fact or theoretical science. And science fiction writ-ers have often predicted changes in our lives decades before those changes arrived.

In his syndicated column (February 6, 2011) "No Clue Where We're Going," Leonard Pitts, Jr., marvels at the trans-formations in our lives since 1860, then 1961. "The point being, we have experienced—are experiencing—greater change at a faster pace than ever before," he wrote. "But as a fish in water doesn't know it's wet, we, living through this challenging, disorienting, 'tectonic' shifting of everything, don't always appreciate the blinding speed with which it is happening. . . . We are too busy bailing water from the sinking boats of former lives and professions. We are too busy trying to define the curve of the new horizon, as familiar old media, modes, models and mores die with bewildering suddenness and new ones snap to life faster still."

His words are well said. And, traditionally, science fiction is well equipped to turn those changes into spirited storytelling.

41. Sartre and the Nothingness of Being

Now when I say "I," it seems hollow to me.
—Jean-Paul Sartre, *Nausea*

I am still persuaded that the hypothesis of a transcendental subject is useless and disastrous. . . . Consciousness is a being, the nature of which is to be conscious of the nothingness of its being. . . . Nothingness lies coiled in the heart of being—like a worm. . . . Man is a useless passion.
—Sartre, *Being and Nothingness*

For poetic vagueness and linguistic extravagance, this is in the best of German traditions. . . . It is as though one were to turn Dostoevsky's novels into philosophic text-books.
—Bertrand Russell on Sartre
in *Wisdom of the West*

My kind of writer is always open to and interested in intellectual history in the West and East, and all points on the compass where our contemporaries, predecessors, and ancestors have grappled with the perennial questions of the human experience. I've always found Sartre to be of interest. One might say that Buddhism begins where existentialism, particularly Sartrean existentialism, ends. Or breaks off. In the West, I think European man's experience as expressed by existentialism can be regarded as a first step on the path that Shakyamuni Buddha walked 2,500 years earlier. No, I am not saying that Sartre was Buddhist. From what I can tell, Eastern philosophies and religions never appeared on his radar screen. But the similarities between Sartre's description of nothingness and the Buddhist definitions for emptiness or the Void are simply too striking, numerous, tantalizing, and begging for comparison to ignore. The Buddhist experience is simply the human experience. (If, as Sartre wrote, "Existentialism is a humanism," then the same can be said of the Buddhadharma.) Therefore, the wisdom that one finds in the Dharma will naturally arise wherever human beings are, East or West, in the distant past (See Marcus Aurelius's *Meditations*), the present, or the future. These claims are broad and sweeping, I know. So let me unpack them more slowly.

Jean-Paul Sartre, a genius, was many things, among them the 1964 laureate of the Nobel Prize in Literature, which he refused to accept. His gifts as an artist (novelist, playwright, essayist) and thinker (he was truly a "public intellectual" and activist) are such that he defies conventional categorizations. Heavily, the influence of Husserl, Heidegger, and (later) Hegel (to name only a few) erupts on his pages. He is both the poster boy for existentialism and an original if sometimes flawed phenomenologist. As an existentialist, his journey to the discovery that consciousness is nothingness takes him through Nietzsche (God is dead) and Kierkegaard (in a world of such uncertainty, man must make a "leap of faith"). But it is as a phenomenologist critiquing and challenging Husserl's Transcendental Ego (which many later phenomenologists regard as a kind of cop-out, a slip back into Berkeleyan idealism; Sartre himself felt Husserl was unfaithful to his own conception of phenomenology, fell into merely being a phenomenalist, and in his account of human existence made it bodiless and sexless, problems that Sartre and Merleau-Ponty corrected by presenting consciousness as embodied) that he achieves an insight perfectly compatible with the Dharma: namely, that *shūnyatā* (emptiness, the Void) is the fundamental reality for all phenomena, and this revelation makes possible our freedom at any moment. What Sartre experienced on the most intense personal level (dramatized in his novels and plays), and as a phenomenologist, is that the self, the personality, the *I* is merely a construct spun from words and concepts—like any other object onto which we project our layers of interpretations or "conceptual paint," as Bhikkhu Bodhi puts it. In *The Phenomenological Movement: A Historical Introduction* (volume two), Herbert Spiegelberg writes:

> While Sartre admits that whenever we reflect upon an experience we always find it associated with an experiencing "I," he claims that in the unreflected experience, for instance that of reading a book, all that is given is the book and its characters but without the reading "I." . . . Sartre's main reason for denying the "I" transcendental status is that he finds it to be unnecessary and hence useless, a reason which sounds more like the logic of Occam's razor than like phenomenology.

It also sounds, I should note, like David Hume's denial of the self's existence. What all this means is that there is no original text for anything, as Sartre's character Roquentin realizes in the novel *Nausea*. There are no certainties. There is no safety net. For Sartre, this nothingness, this emptiness, is initially the occasion for despair or nausea. How shall we act—how shall we live—in a world where everything is so unsubstantial? Where the bourgeois (white and black and otherwise) lives blindly—and inauthentically—within the presuppositions of the Natural Attitude, engaging in "bad faith" because it believes its fictitious constructs to be real. As Roquentin observes in Sartre's novel:

> And just what is Antoine Roquentin? An abstraction. A pale reflection of myself wavers in my consciousness. Antoine Roquentin . . . and suddenly the "I" pales, and fades out. Lucid, static, forlorn, consciousness is walled-up; it perpetuates itself. Nobody lives there any more . . . the diversity of things, their individuality, were only an appearance, a veneer. . . . I understood that I had found the key to Existence, the key to my Nausea, to my own life. In fact, all that I could grasp beyond that returns to this fundamental absurdity. . . . The world of explanations and reasons is not the world of existence. . . .

In Sartre's cycle of novels, *The Roads to Freedom*, the character Mathieu Delarue comes to a similar conclusion: "Everything is outside. . . . Inside, nothing, not even a puff of smoke, there is no *inside*, there is nothing. Myself: nothing. I am free." Given the nothingness of consciousness, we are *condemned* to be free in a world that, sans God, is necessarily *absurd*, where the only meaning we find is the meaning that we ourselves have the courage to create. As a young man in my late teens and early twenties, the existentialist vision exerted a powerful influence on my thoughts, and on the way I interpreted what was happening around me (the civil rights, then Black Power movements; that influence is surely the reason I made Chaym Smith such an existential character in *Dreamer*). Our social world—and especially the world of racial experience—abounds in examples of bad faith and essentialism (racial, gender, nationalistic, ethnic), where men and women flee from reality (for example, that racial identity is an illusion); from the fact that "existence precedes essence"; from facing the fact that, moment by moment, we *choose* our lives and the meaning of our lives (the final meaning for which will not be determined until our death, when we can act no more, when we become, as Alfred North Whitehead put it, no longer Subjective Aims but instead Eternal Objects). But where the experience of nothingness for Sartre led to despair and nausea, the experience of *shūnyatā* for a Buddhist is the occasion for joy; it is a guarantee that we can change and eventually realize liberation from suffering. The lack of ontological foundation that leads to Sartre seeing the world as absurd leads in the East to two thousand years of robust Buddhist humor based on that very absurdity, especially in the Zen traditions. (In *Being and Nothingness*, Sartre puts it this way: "It follows that my freedom is the unique foundation of values and that *nothing*, absolutely nothing, justifies me in adopting this or that particular value, this or that particular scale of values. As a being by whom values exist, I am unjustifiable. My freedom is anguished at being the foundation of values while itself without foundation.") And where Roquentin feels that in an absurd world where there is no reason for doing any one thing rather than another, a Buddhist guided by the Eight-Fold Path and Bodhisattva vow knows that "one thing" will cause suffering to oneself and others while "another" will not. For Buddhism, man cannot be a "useless passion," for the Dharma teaches us how to understand desire and passion, and how to master them, as opposed to desire and passion exerting mastery over us. Sartre's philosophical vision is rife with problems. Spiegelberg points out, "In general Sartre is apt to begin with descriptive analyses but to push them in the direction of hermeneutic interpretations far beyond what immediate inspection would seem to warrant." He had a fondness for paradoxical formulations, some of them probably influenced by Hegelian dialectics. His embrace of Marxism (with its assumptions and presuppositions) is often at war with his positions as an existentialist. His personal idiosyncrasies often impair his analyses—for example, Sartre's famous "look," or gaze that fixes the Other, has about it the tincture of being a threat; why not instead, Spiegelberg notes, use for analysis the "look" one receives from a friend or loved one? (And another experience Sartre was fond of using as an example was "shame.") One might say, as I have on occasion, that the Thing (*en-soi*)—or things of the world—frightened Sartre with their opacity and viscosity and his feeling that they would completely overwhelm consciousness (*pour-soi*). By contrast, Maurice Merleau-Ponty (Sartre's competitor of sorts) does not present problems of this kind, and is a much more careful, reliable, and convincing phenomenologist. Much has been published in recent decades about the thematic overlaps and interplay between the philosophy of existentialism and the philosophy of Buddhism. That comparative study still remains fertile ground for exploration.

42. The Truth-Telling Power
of Fiction

*If literature isn't everything, it's not worth a single
hour of someone's trouble.*

—Jean-Paul Sartre

Whenever we discuss literature it is likely that at some point
we find the conversation turning to its sister disciple, philosophy. Both forms of expression offer interpretations of
our experience delivered through the performance of language. Moreover, the relationship between philosophy and
literature is reinforced by the obvious but seldom-stated fact
that philosophers are not just thinkers; they are also writers. And our finest storytellers, the ones who transform and
deepen our understanding of the world, are not just writers;
they, too, are engaged in the adventure of ideas, to borrow
a phrase from Alfred North Whitehead. But, unfortunately,
our conversation on this important subject is often clouded
by prejudices and misconceptions about the nature of philosophy and literary art—for example, that writers tell stories (mere fiction) but philosophers tell the truth. However,
I think the very creative process that characterizes literary
art of the highest order may, if viewed from the *inside*, clarify some aspects of this relationship, and demystify the algo-

rithms of creativity in composition that apply to both fiction and philosophy.

It's worth saying at the outset that French storytellers and philosophers stretching back to Descartes and Voltaire have long recognized the intimate relationship between philosophy and literature. Descartes, the first modern philosopher, explained that he chose a first-person, literary or narrative approach (with a very compelling conflict) for his *Meditations on First Philosophy* in order to render that work more accessible to readers, specifically to women, and in that endeavor he was hugely successful, for Queen Christina sent a warship to bring him to Sweden so he could teach her philosophy at the dreadful hour of five in the morning, as I dramatized in my story "The Queen and the Philosopher." But outside the Gallic sensibility on the Continent, and half a century ago in America, the complementariness of art as knowledge and philosophy as a rigorous art form was still underappreciated.

In fact, forty years ago there was outright hostility, mainly among some analytic philosophers, to the idea that philosophy and literature have any relationship at all. (And the analytic tradition is, of course, dominant in American philosophy departments.) This lack of appreciation was so much the case in the 1970s that when I was a graduate student and novelist working on my doctorate, I copied into my writer's notebook at the time a quote from a letter Schiller sent to Goethe, which I found myself identifying with, even though it is based on a rather odd instance of experiential apartheid. He said, "My understanding works more in a symbolizing method, and thus I hover, as a hybrid, between ideas and perceptions, between law and feeling, between a technical mind and genius . . . The poetic mind generally got the better of me when I ought to have philosophized, and my philosophical mind when I wished to poeticize."

Professor Michael Boylan at Marymount University, my

co-author for the book *Philosophy: An Innovative Introduction: Fictive Narrative, Primary Texts, and Responsive Writing*, earned his PhD at the University of Chicago. In one of his recent essays, Professor Boylan recalled that "there were some philosophers at Chicago who encouraged the intersection of fiction and philosophy, including Paul Ricoeur and Arthur Adkins, [but] the general attitude was that I should keep my passion for fiction a secret. . . . Real philosophers," he was told, "were interested only in making claims through the analysis of language, logic, and science."

Boylan's lament, and also that of Schiller, with its categorical separation between ideas and perceptions and the problematic and erroneous dualism he establishes between law and feeling, captures in a way part of the difficulty we have had in our grappling with the relationship between philosophy and literature since the eighteenth century. Some of the problem arises because of our respect for the methods found in the empirical sciences. In 1953, the Yale professor Brand Blanshard, who *did* deeply appreciate the rigor required for good writing, eloquently broached these misgivings in his Adamson Lecture at Manchester University, which became a lovely little book entitled *On Philosophical Style*:

"Philosophizing proper," he wrote, "is a purely intellectual enterprise. Its business is to analyze fundamental assumptions, such as that all events have causes; and to fit the conclusions together in a coherent view of nature and man's place in it. [It] is pledged to discuss these issues with scientific detachment and dispassionateness. . . . Philosophy is not an attempt to excite or entertain; it is not an airing of one's prejudices—the philosopher is supposed to have no prejudices; it is not an attempt to tell a story, or paint a picture, or to get anyone to do anything, or to make anyone like this and dislike that." But then shortly after this statement Blanshard acknowledged, "Philosophy, while an impersonal subject, is thought and written by persons. The brains of these persons, when they think, are not dynamos humming in a vacuum; actual thought is always bathed in personal feeling, and invested with the lights and shades of an individual temperament."

Some philosophers have seen feeling and the techniques of literary craftsmanship as being dangerous. Using concrete examples or empirical content, said Blanshard, can be risky because concrete things are complex, and if you offer one as an example, you might pick out the wrong point in it. In other words, things mean *too* much. Kant was so convinced this would happen that, for the most part, he deliberately avoided using illustrations. And in *Anthropology from a Pragmatic Point of View*, he wrote that "to be subject to emotions and passions is probably always an illness of mind because both emotion and passion exclude the sovereignty of reason." Opposing this view, Blanshard argued that "no philosopher is or can be a disembodied cerebrum; what he is called on to exclude is not all emotions but only irrelevant emotions." Futhermore, he emphasized that "to write and think clearly is to give every statement a reference to one distinct fact of sense perception . . . because if we cannot convert our generalizations on call into statements about particular instances, that does show in nine cases out of ten that we are not yet clear as to what precisely we are trying to say."

And for Blanshard, the safest feeling of all in thinking and writing philosophy is the "love of truth." He says that this love of truth, with its transparent honesty and objectivity of mind, is "wanting to see the facts as they are, to follow the argument where it leads, even if it leads to the painful flouting of one's other wants, the readiness to consider all evidence, to give full weight to objections, to believe and admit that one has been wrong."

Finally, Blanshard summed up his conception of the philosophical enterprise with a quote from William James, who described philosophy as "a peculiarly stubborn effort to think clearly." So stubborn, Blanshard notes, that "whenever he [James] was engaged in any considerable piece of literary composition his letters to his friends grew full of groaning over the slowness and arduousness of his progress. He assures them that working all day and rewriting half a dozen times has only yielded him a page and a half of manuscript. . . . 'Everything comes out wrong with me at first,' he said, 'but when once objectified in a crude shape, I can torture and poke and scrape and pat it till it offends me no more.'"

I'd like to dwell for a moment on why William James did so much groaning, and why his writing was so slow, for it is here that a common dimension of writing for the storyteller and the philosopher is revealed. And let me dare to begin with the ambiguity inherent in a personal anecdote:

Many years ago, when my daughter was in high school, she competed in a talent contest sponsored by the NAACP. I drove her to this event, and just before it started, I found myself chatting with another father, one of my brothers in Sigma Pi Phi, a professional fraternity for black men started by W. E. B. Du Bois over a century ago. He is a lawyer, and his daughter was also competing that day. As we waited for the contest to begin, he told me that he enjoyed my novel *Middle Passage*. I thanked him, and mentioned that I appreciated his reading the story, because over a period of six years I threw away 3,000 pages to arrive at the 250-page book he experienced. I watched his eyes grow wide. When I said my ratio of throwaway to kept pages is often 20:1, I saw his mouth fall open. Then I realized that he probably thought the pages he read sprang almost fully formed from my brain like Athena from the head of Zeus. He might even have imagined, wrongly, that when I started writing *Middle Passage*, I knew how the story would turn out.

There was no way he could know that for me a novel is a

very special thought experiment, because I've always seen the literary as a potential site for philosophical agency. And I've never seen ideas as existing in some abstract realm floating high above human experience. Rather, I see ideas as originating in the historical muck and mud of our daily experience, cloaked in the immediate particulars of this world, and only later do we abstract them for the purpose of study and reflection. So what does this philosophical novelist do? I simply try to return those ideas to the palpable world of experience from which they first sprang. This approach is not different from what Hilary Putnam suggested in his 1978 book, *Meaning and the Moral Science*, where he said, "the novel aids us in the imaginative re-creation of moral perplexities, in the widest sense." If philosophy is direct discourse, then fiction, as Michael Boylan has long argued, can be seen not as play or frivolity but possibly as a form of indirect discourse that makes claims or judgments about this world and how it works.

Something I'm sure my fraternity brother didn't know was that Ernest Hemingway rewrote the last page of *A Farewell to Arms* thirty-nine times. Literary art is founded foursquare on exactly this painstaking process of revision, trial, and error—or *re*envisioning. And on the humility and openness involved in—as Blanshard put it—"wanting to see the facts as they are"; to follow the (fictional) argument where it leads, even to the painful flouting of one's other wants (which might be the story one at first wanted to write); the readiness to consider all evidence, to give full weight to objections (from those reading one's pages when they are in progress), to believe and admit that one has been wrong (in the earlier drafts of a work). Literary art, then, is first and foremost an art form concerned with James's "peculiarly stubborn effort to think clearly," and also—because it is literature—it aims for the most sophisticated and memorable performance of language.

I'm not talking about escapist entertainments, or your garden-variety novel with flat, unvoiced language bereft of vividness, metaphor, and simile; or commercial or formula fiction usually written within two years or less with paint-by-numbers plots. I'm not talking about utilitarian prose as uninteresting as what we hear in the supermarket or at the DMV. Crafting language takes time, because writing well *is* exactly the same thing as thinking well, and that requires time to *re*think one's options and alternatives at every moment in a prose passage. *Techne is* vision, a form of truth. Style *is* sense. Each page is a prayer. This is so for two reasons. First, because language antedates every writer. As Sartre explained, "Language is a nature when I discover it within myself and outside myself with its resistances and laws which escape me: words have affinities and customs that I must *observe*, must *learn*. . . ." And the second reason is because literary art demands specificity and granularity of detail, what the philosopher Duns Scotus called *haecceitas* (the "thisness" of things) and what the poet Gerard Manley Hopkins referred to as "inscape." (I would also argue that it demands narrative generosity, a giving by the writer of more than is simply required to fulfill a particular literary task.) To achieve this, every aspect of a well-wrought story must be scrutinized hundreds, if not thousands, of times, for as Prosper Mérimée said, "In fiction there must be a theoretical basis to the most minute details. Even a single glove must have its theory."

Fiction writers (and William James) find this process arduous as they try to wrest novelty from the "resistances" that Sartre understood to be so recalcitrant, because precision in the shaping of language requires sustaining for days, months, and even years that most difficult and often fatiguing of conscious activities: our *full* attention. T. S. Eliot in his *Four Quartets* expressed the problem this way:

Words strain,
Crack and sometimes break, under the burden,
Under the tension, slip, slide, perish,
Decay with imprecision, will not stay in place,
Will not stay still.

And Eliot concludes that poetry is

. . . a raid on the inarticulate
With shabby equipment always deteriorating
In the general mess of imprecision and feeling . . .

When we examine the presence of the word, we find,
if we are phenomenologists, the Other. Others who have
used a word, who left their sweat and palm oil on it, who
invested the word with multiple meanings, thereby creating
a horizon of sense that we shall never—*ever*—reach. Furthermore, and contrary to Kant, emotion and passion prop-
erly understood *do* serve reason. Concepts have an affective
quality, an emotional or feeling tone (the compound German word for this is *Begriffsgefuhl*) just as feelings in the
Heideggerean sense disclose an analytic dimension—that is,
they bring forth profiles of the world that are meaningful, so
that these two experiences—ideas and feelings—cannot be
as easily separated or segregated as Schiller believed. Taking
this a step further, J. Lowenberg, writing about Hegel's dia-
lectic, reminded us, "Ideas and beliefs, too, may be preten-
tious, pedantic, fantastic, bizarre, grotesque, inept, perverse,
reckless, blind, and blatant."

But the word is just the first linguistic dimension that a
writer must despoil. He must also consider another larger
unit of reason and expression: the package or quantum of
experience we call the paragraph. "Rhythm," Blanshard
stated in his lecture, "is one of the subtlest of all instruments

in the delicate work of conveying thought." Each sentence is a unit of energy, something we realize when we hear a writer read his or her work out loud, or if an actor performs it. When writing well, one works very hard at creating a musical variety in sentence length, in sentence forms, and throughout a paragraph; at chopping away waste; at harmoniously blending the final sentence of one paragraph with the first sentence of the next through rhythm and rhetorical techniques; at revising until a sentence surprises and is no longer recognizable as its first-draft incarnation. These are not things most readers like my fraternity brother will see, nor should they, for craft should be experienced the way we do our spectacles or contact lenses, as something that enables us to see while not calling attention to itself. Again, this process requires time, which commercial writers and journalists simply do not have, since revision is an almost endless exercise in cutting away (like sculpting the sentence or paragraph from stone) and also a constant layering of the language (like working with the sentence as you would clay).

I can't emphasize enough the importance of this layering process. In it we see what Sartre meant when he said in *Saint Genet* that "words sometimes display surprising independence, marrying in defiance of all laws and thus producing puns and oracles within language." It is precisely those unexpected oracles, those surprises and discoveries that a writer hopes to stumble upon.

It goes without saying that, unlike Kant, one eagerly embraces the possibilities of illustration, concreteness, and especially metaphor. Absent the possibilities of metaphor, we would not have that perfect fusion of ontology and epistemology called Plato's Myth of the Cave, Schopenhauer's parable of the porcupines, the fables of Aesop, the parables of Jesus, the Buddhist Jātaka tales, Franz Kafka's "The Metamorphosis," John Gardner's *Grendel*, Ralph Ellison's *Invisible Man*, George Orwell's *Animal Farm*, my story "Menagerie," Richard Wright's "The Man Who Lived Underground," or a film like *They Shoot Horses, Don't They?*

Yet even after all these linguistic considerations, what I sometimes call applied aesthetics, the work of a fiction writer who loves truth and is pledged to honor James's "peculiarly stubborn effort to think clearly" by logically tracing all the implications for actions that proceed convincingly and inexorably from beginning to middle to end, as well as creating a language performance with subtext and nuance, has only just begun.

In order to tell a story, one must have a plot. And creating an elegant, original, efficient plot that keeps a writer, then a reader, in a state of suspense, constantly probing and asking the right questions, is always a difficult challenge for the novelist or short fiction writer who refuses to rely on the formulas associated with genre fiction, or on political ideology, kitsch, or preestablished meanings. Plot, the scaffolding in every story, should be of great interest to every philosopher (and reader) because, according to John Gardner, who knew a few things about writing, "Plot is the writer's equivalent to the philosopher's argument." Eighty-six years ago, in *Aspects of the Novel*, a now classic series of lectures, E. M. Forster drew a distinction between story and plot that is still useful to us today:

> Let us define plot. We have defined a story as a narrative of events arranged in their time-sequence. A plot is also a narrative of events, the emphasis falling on causality. "The king died, and then the queen died" is a story. "The king died, and then the queen died of grief" is a plot. The time-sequence is preserved, but the sense of causality overshadows it. Or again: "The queen died,

no one knew why, until it was discovered that it was through grief at the death of the king." This is a plot with a mystery in it, a form capable of high development. It suspends the time-sequence, it moves as far away from the story as its limitations will allow. Consider the death of the queen. If it is in a story we say "and then?" If it is in a plot we ask "why?" That is the fundamental difference between these two aspects of the novel.

The question we ask of plot—"why"—is akin to the question we ask in philosophy. Both literature and philosophy begin with wonder. In an interrogative mode. Even more important, the question reminds us that we think and organize our experience in narratives; specifically the left hemisphere of our brain does that. In his book *The Ethical Brain*, Michael Gazzaniga, a pioneer in cognitive neuroscience, says, "The left hemisphere makes strange input logical, it includes a special region that interprets the inputs we receive every moment and weaves them into stories to form the ongoing narrative of our self-image and our beliefs. I call this area of the left hemisphere the interpreter because it seeks explanations for internal and external events and expands on the actual facts we experience to make sense of, or interpret, the events of our life."

Narrative, then, is one way we are hardwired for interpreting temporal events, and it is what Plato meant in the *Timaeus* when he spoke of even our scientific explanations being a "likely story." In other words, our explanations for this mysterious universe we inhabit are just that—"likely," though not absolute. And they are always provisional, subject to revision based on new evidence. (We should also remember, as so many people have pointed out, that Plato chose for his dialogues a form that is by its very nature dramatic.)

But even after exerting that control over a complex story, a mountain of work still remains. Each and every character detail and description, each prop on the page of the fiction, must be scrutinized hundreds of times for its effect and accuracy. If a dramatic scene is richly evoked, placing us so thoroughly within its ambience that we forget the room we're sitting in or fail to hear the telephone ring; if in it we can "see" the "thisness" of every carefully described object on the fictional stage; if our senses imaginatively respond to, say, the quality of late-afternoon light as it falls upon the characters, and to imagery evoking smells, sounds, and tastes; if each revealing, moment-by-moment action, feeling, utterance, pause, and sigh of the characters is microscopically tracked and reverentially recorded by the writer, who, like an actor, must psychologically inhabit *all* the characters at every moment in that scene; if every significant nuance of that densely textured scene is present with almost a palpable feel on the page, then it is because the writer has made thousands of intelligent interpretative decisions in any successful story to achieve coherence, consistency, and completeness, which are the same criteria we use for evaluating works of philosophy.

In his *Notebooks* (1935–42), Albert Camus, who earned in 1936 his *diplôme d'études supérieures* (an equivalent to our master's degree), notoriously said, "Feelings and images multiply a philosophy by ten. People think only in images. . . . If you want to be a philosopher, write novels." A few philosophers have wisely heeded this advice—William Gass, George Santayana, Rebecca Goldstein, Michael Boylan, and Iris Murdoch, to name just a few. They understood the risks and rewards of embracing the natural kinship of storytelling and philosophy. Yet in the interest of honesty, and to paraphrase Professor Boylan, I must say that what we *lose* when philosophy takes the form of storytelling is exact precision in the presentation of a claim; but what we *gain* through the techniques and tools of a literature that is richly imagined and deeply felt is, as Blanshard argued, the ability to uniquely engage an audience's intellect, emotions, and imagination in their fullness—the "everything" that Sartre felt literature (and perhaps also philosophy) should be.

Afterword
Notes from a Former Student

MARC C. CONNER

I have been privileged to encounter the work of Charles Johnson in a number of ways: as a student in his fiction writing
seminars at the University of Washington in the late 1980s; as
a scholar of his work since the late 1990s, publishing numerous reviews, papers, and articles, and also my book of essays
on his work, *Charles Johnson: The Novelist as Philosopher*;
and as a teacher of his novels, short stories, and philosophical
writings in my literature courses. But although I've written
often about his work from multiple literary and philosophical perspectives, I've never addressed—nor have I ever heard
anyone else address—the activity that has probably occu-
pied more of his time over the last thirty-plus years than any
other: the teaching of writing.

Yet it's peculiarly appropriate to talk of Charles Johnson as
simultaneously a writer and a teacher of writing, for this gets
at two of the fundamental elements of his identity. He is, first
and foremost, a writer—and he is by profession (or was, until
his official retirement in June 2009) a teacher of other writers.
But he goes further: Johnson is a theorist of the pedagogies
of writing, or, put differently, he has thought long and hard
about what we do when we teach others to write. And he has

227

pursued the question that nags many of us: Why—*why on earth?*—do we teach people to write? What motivates this?

Johnson himself was never a product of the university writing workshop approach to teaching writing. He first *taught himself* how to write, having written six novels in the late 1960s and early 1970s, cranking them out at the rate of one novel per ten-week college term—a rate that at least speaks to his work ethic and determination. He then came under the tutelage of the late John Gardner, and so underwent a second level of education in the teaching of writing. Finally, in 1976, Johnson came to the University of Washington to teach writing at the college level, and so he learned to teach writing through the necessity of having to do it on a daily basis. Through these very different experiences in his own learning, Johnson developed his own idiosyncratic method, what he calls his "boot camp" in creative writing.

The best way to describe these fiction workshops run by Johnson is as an all-consuming immersion for the students in the many techniques and skills required to become an accomplished writer of good prose fiction. In a 2003 essay for the *Chronicle of Higher Education*, Johnson describes what he emphasizes in these courses: it is "a labor-intensive 'skill acquisition' course"—he says he is less interested in *what* one writes than in *how* one writes; it must include "capacious" reading and instruction in all styles, genres, and subgenres of fiction; it must train students in a large "repertoire of literary strategies," including the mastery of dozens of writing exercises culled from figures such as Gardner, Weathers, and Winchester, and many of Johnson's own invention; students must begin reading a full dictionary—must learn to keep a writer's journal—must outline a half dozen future stories—and much more. The goal, he states, is for them to master as much as possible the techniques and skills—the toolbox—of fiction writing.

This method is most akin to the medieval apprentice model, whereby one progresses from novice to trainee to journeyman to—if one has sufficient gifts—master's level. Johnson compares it quite rightly to the training undergone by a jazz musician or a martial artist. For just as the beginner martial artist must master certain basic stances, blocks, and strikes, and then progress into basic kata forms that themselves will become increasingly complex as the student grows, and only then can the student begin to understand how to apply the kata training in actual combat—so, too, the beginner artist must move through basic techniques into more advanced forms. And just as the martial arts adage holds that a student must perform a move at least a thousand times before he has made it his own, and at least ten thousand times before he can use it naturally in combat, so, too, the writer must repeat and repeat the basic moves of her craft before it becomes her own and can be employed in creating publishable fiction— the writer's equivalent, perhaps, of tournament sparring . . . or even real-life fighting?

Yet the training of dozens of prose technicians each year hardly describes Charles Johnson's total efforts as a teacher of writing. In another essay, "Storytelling and the Alpha Narrative," he states that "craft is only one side of the story," and that "the *other* side of the story—what craft is in the service of"—is even more compelling. "Why," he asks, "do we write fiction? Why do we read it? . . . Why are stories so important to us?" It's because this question is so consuming for Johnson that he also has his fiction students read such works as Longinus's classic aesthetics treatise *On the Sublime*, along with Sartre's probing essay "What Is Literature?," Albert Murray's "The Hero and the Blues," and Northrop Frye's elegant study *The Educated Imagination*. The goal is to help students understand the majesty and magic of deep reading experiences. Johnson argues that the true practice of read-

ing has much in common with the phenomenological practice of bracketing one's experience and focusing only on the present moment—much as the Buddhist turns all attention to this present spot of existence and resists the allure of the illusionary past and future. Johnson blocks out all extra-literary concerns—critical ideas, reputations, literary theories, and so on—and seeks only "the same innocent enchantment I had when I was a reader of twelve or thirteen . . . the experience of mystery and wonder, and needing to know *what happens next.*" When a story has sufficient power and magic to so consume the reader that everything disappears except the story—this is what Johnson terms an "Alpha Narrative": "stories that endure," that "liberate our perception." Or more simply: "whopping good stories."

How does one create such a story? Johnson suggests that it is less a matter of conscious creation, more a matter of allowing the story to emerge, much like the old Zen proverb of the sculptor whose main task is to see the stunning statue that resides within the unworked piece of wood or stone (a figure he depicts in Reb the coffinmaker in his novel *Oxherding Tale*). Johnson cites Aristotle in this regard and his concept of *energeia*, or "the actualization of the potential that exists in character and situation." "The actualization of the potential"—so a skilled writer must be able, first, to recognize a great story when it appears before her (thus Johnson's insistence on training their skills as readers); and that writer must have the *techne* necessary to help that story emerge into a work of serious craftsmanship, perhaps even art. He writes, "I view the techniques and elements of craft that I've taught writing students simply as tools to prepare them for the time when such a narrative drops into their laps."

All of these ideas—of the reading experience, of the craft and techniques of writing, of the range of voices, styles, and perspectives that the writer must master—are present

Afterword

in Johnson's own creative work, as any reader of his novels and stories can attest. Of particular interest to me is the venture that he began over fifteen years ago, writing a "Bedtime Story" for the Humanities Washington annual autumn gathering. These stories are incredibly diverse, in every sense of the word—including its Renaissance meaning of "not alike in nature or qualities" or even "different from, or opposed to what is right, good . . . *perverse, adverse,*" particularly if we understand "what is right" as "what our culture today tells us is right." To the standards of today's culture, with its emphasis on hedonism, mediocrity, a flattening of experience and of art, and particularly its moral indifference, Johnson's work is certainly *adverse, perverse.* This is the heart of his teacher John Gardner's credo, *On Moral Fiction*—that fiction calls us to an ethical stance, demands that we engage our moral lives, what Levinas terms the face-to-face confrontation with the other. These imaginative, fanciful stories of bedtime are indeed confrontations with otherness: fairy tales of princes turning to frogs, historical meditations on Descartes's meeting with the Queen of Sweden, imaginative journeys to Africa or Ancient Greece, science fiction forays; and they exhibit all the formal diversity of an eighteenth-century narrative, ranging from animal tale to parable to fabula to dream vision to good old-fashioned realism. The best of these stories, for this reader, is "Dr. King's Refrigerator," a delightful reimagining of the early days of King's work, focusing more on King as man, husband, and philosopher, less on the world historical figure he would shortly become. The story delights and instructs, in the best Horatian tradition, but also in the tradition of the book of Proverbs, a text that has fascinated Johnson for more than a decade. Proverbs is the domain of wisdom literature, the teachings that allow a people to survive in the midst of a world that would consume them. If modernity teaches us to disavow a literature that teaches, Johnson insists that only a literature that does teach is finally worthy of our attention. This is his phenomenology of teaching, as all distraction fades and the reader is left in the solitary confrontation with the transcendent written word. To read, to ponder, to create, and to help others in these tasks, this is the word-work of Charles Johnson, and our participation in this exercise is, to me, the most telling tribute we can offer to this superb writer.

An earlier version of this essay was first delivered at the 2010 American Writers and Poets conference at a panel dedicated to the work of Charles Johnson, and subsequently printed in Nibir K. Ghosh and E. Ethelbert Miller's book *Charles Johnson: Embracing the World.*

Acknowledgments

I want to thank poet E. Ethelbert Miller for making this book possible by asking me a year's worth of probing questions about the craft of writing for his E-Channel project, and Washington and Lee University provost and literary scholar Marc Conner for providing me with the file for those essay/posts when I needed them. I am also profoundly indebted to John Glynn for his brilliant, sustained editorial work and crucial help with shaping the manuscript at every stage of its development. I am equally indebted to longtime Scribner president Susan Moldow and publicist Jessica Yu for their wisdom and outstanding professionalism and, of course, to photographer Zorn B. Taylor. As always, I must thank Joan, my wife of forty-six years, and our children for grounding my life and work as an artist, writer, and philosopher.